PARENT-TEACHER SHELF

Please check all items for damages
before leaving the Library.
Thereafter you will be held
responsible for all injuries
to items beyond reasonable wear.

Helen M. Plum Memorial Library

Lombard, Illinois

A daily fine will be charged for
overdue materials.

JAN   2010

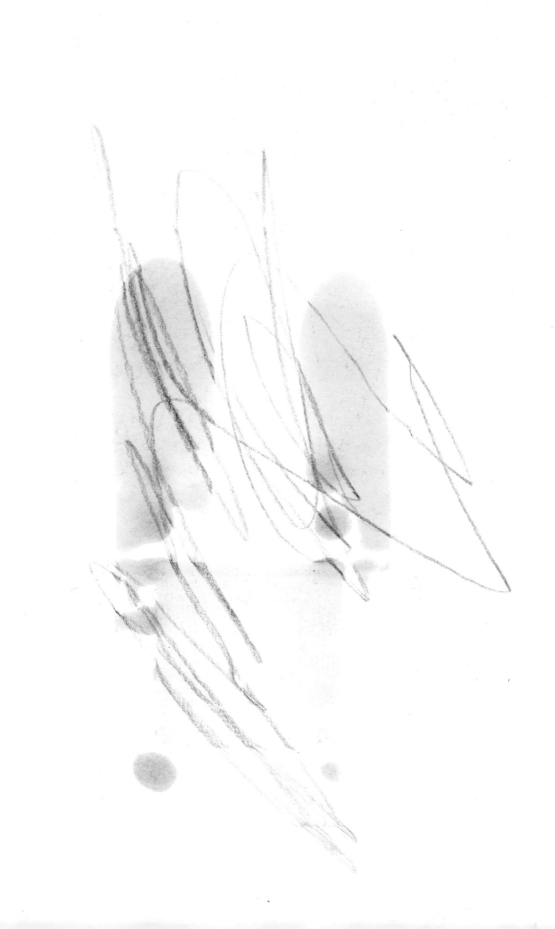

My Body

Sally Hewitt
Angela Royston

FIREFLY BOOKS

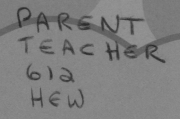

A FIREFLY BOOK

Published by Firefly Books Ltd. 2009
Copyright © 2008 QEB Publishing, Inc.

First Printing

Publisher Cataloging-in-Publication Data (U.S.)

Hewitt, Sally, 1949-
   My body : a fun way to find out all the facts about your body / Sally Hewitt.
[160] p. : col. photos., ill. ; cm.
Includes index.
Summary: Addresses basic questions about the human body asked by children.
Topics include the heart, memory, bones.
ISBN-13: 978-1-55407-522-5
ISBN-10: 1-55407-522-X
1. Human body--Juvenile literature. I. Title.
612 dc22   QP37.H495 2009

Library and Archives Canada Cataloguing in Publication

Hewitt, Sally, 1949-
   My body : a fun way to find out all the facts about your body / Sally
Hewitt, Angela Royston.
Includes index.
ISBN-13: 978-1-55407-522-5
ISBN-10: 1-55407-522-X
   1. Human body--Juvenile literature. 2. Human physiology--Juvenile
literature. I. Royston, Angela II. Title.

Published in the United States by
Firefly Books (U.S.) Inc.
P.O. Box 1338, Ellicott Station
Buffalo, New York 14205

Published in Canada by
Firefly Books Ltd.
66 Leek Crescent
Richmond Hill, Ontario L4B 1H1

Printed and bound in Singapore

Authors Sally Hewitt and Angela Royston
Consultant Terry Jennings
Project Editor Judith Millidge
Designers Kim Hall and Louise Downey
Illustrator Chris Davidson

Publisher Steve Evans
Creative Director Zeta Davies
Managing Editor Amanda Askew

Picture credits
Key: t=top, b=bottom, m=middle, l=left, r=right

Alamy Bubbles Photolibrary 15, Jim Zuckerman 39, Jupiterimages-Polka Dot 51t, Jason Smalley-Wildscape 81t, Bubbles Photolibrary 115r, Don Smith 140

Corbis Daniel Attia /Zefa 18, Jim Craigmyle 22, Gareth Brown 28–29, Emely/ zefa 30, Christian Liewig 38, Jennie Woodcock-Reflections Photolibrary 53r, Virgo Productions–Zefa 53l, Barbara Peacock 61b, Sam Diephuis/zefa 86–87, Norbert Schaefer 90, LWA-Dann Tardif 95b, Brigitte Sporrer/zefa/97t, Lisa B 100t, Randy Faris 100b, Heide Benser/zefa 101t, Creasource 104b Anna Peisl/zefa 125r, Tom Stewart 144

Dorling Kindersley Susanna Price 136b, Andy Crawford and Steve Gorton 137, 142t

Getty Images Mel Yates 10, Stephen Frink 17, Kevin Mackintosh 20, Erik Dreyer 28t, Barbara Peacock 51t, Karen Moskowitz 57bl, Joe Major 73b, Steve Shott 96, Lonnie Duka 102, Gala Narezo 104, Tara Moore 105b, Ryan McVay 112l, Seymour Hewitt 116, Camille Tokerud 118, Tim Hall 120r, Atsuko Murano/ailead 125r, Loungepark 129br, Photoshot 142tr, Jamie Gril 145tl, James Hardy 145b

Science Photo Library Mauro Fermariello 14

Shutterstock Wizdata inc 8, Z Adam 8l, Jaimie Duplass 9b, Gelpi 9t, Supri Suharjoto 12, Darren Baker 13, Juriah Mosim 19, paparazzit 26, Gelpi 27l, phdpsx 27r, Serhiy Kyrychenko 29, Arvind Balarama 29b, Julian Rovagnati 29t, JJ pixs 31t, Jacek Chabraszewski 36, David Davis 37t, Jacek Chabraszewski 37br, Losevsky Pavel 39b, Irina Klebanova 35b, Teodor Ostojic 35t, Elena Elisseeva 40, Roberto Kylio 42, Olga LyubKina 42, Julian Rovagnati 42, Kivrins Anatolijs 43b, Graca Victoria 43t, Philip Lange 44t, Serghei Starus 44b, George P Choma 45, Ariusz Nawrocki 46, Andresr 47tl, Gelpi 47m, Kameel4u 47tr, Cindy Minear 48, Jiang Dao Hua 49, JoLin 55b, Jacek Chabraszewski 56, Igor Kisselev 57t, Vinicius Tupinamba 58, Chas 59b, KrisN 59b, Flashon Studio 60, Sharon Day 63b, Robert Spriggs 63b, James Steidl 63t, Tatiana Morozova 64, Vlas2000 65t, Andrjuss 65b, Norberto Lauria 65b, Larisa Lofitskaya 66, Pavel Sazonov 66r, Larisa Lofitskaya 67, Rob Byron 67t, Nobor 68c, Galushko Sergey 68bl, Nuno Garuti 68br, Sergey Peterman 68cl, Ismael Montero Verdu 68cr, Monika23 69tr, Stuart Monk 69t, Scott Rothstein 69b, Sandra Caldwell 70cr, Cen 70tr, Colour 70cl, Chiyacat 70b, Sergieiev 70b, Skazka Grez 70bl, Antonio Munoz Palomares 71, Andrey Armyagov 71t, Gorilla 71b, Dmitriy Shironosov 72, David J Morgan 73b Gualberto Becerra 76l, kameel4u 76r, Gelpi 77, 79b, Olga Shelego 78, Andresr 79t, Elena Elisseeva 79m, Jozsef Szasz-Fabian 81b, Ostanina Vadimovna 82, Claudio Baldini 83mr, Cloki 83br, Creative Images 83ml, Ilya Gridnev 83t, MaxFX 83bl, Merrill Dyck 84, Aurelio 85t, Alexander Shalamov 85b, Matt Antonino 86–87, Leah-Anne Thompson 86t, Tamara KuliKova 87t, Doug Schneider 88, Losevsky Pavel 89b; 89t, Kisalev/Jaime Duplass 91, Maria Wariatka 92, Thomas M Perkins 93t, Jiri Vaclavek 93b, Kisalev Valerevich 94t, Marcel Mooij 95t, Shantell photographe 98, Losevsky Pavel 99b, Monkey Business Images 101b, Alusinya 103b, D Barton 103t, Tatiana Mironenko 105t Losevsky Pavel 94b, Jaimie Duplass 109, Olga LyubKina 110; 111t, Matka Wariatka 111b, Andi Berger 113, Juriah Mosin 114, Herbert Kratky 115, Elena Elisseeva 117;119, Vladimir MelniKov 121, Lorraine Kourafas 124; Larisa Lofitskaya 128, Elena Elisseeva 129t, phdpsx 130b, Robert Spriggs 131b, Suzanne Tucker 131t, Cameramannz 131b, Nassyrov Ruslan 131b, Yummy 132b, tamzinm 132l, Lukacs Racz 132r, Robyn Mackenzie 132c, Ray Hub 132bc, Muriel Lasure 133b, Thomas M Perkins 133t, ryby 134t, Noam Armonn 135t, Renata Osinska 135b, Sebastian Kaulitzki 136t, Uravid 136–137, 3445128471 138, Lana Langlois 138b, Yuri Shirokov 138b, 3445128471 141t, Juriah Mosin 143b

Contents

My Brain

My Digestive System

My Skin

Words in **bold** are explained in
the glossary on page 147.

My Heart and Lungs

What is your heart?

Your heart is a strong **muscle** about the size of your fist. It has two pumps that push your **blood** around your body. Your heart sits just to the left of the middle of your chest.

Your heart never stops working. It pumps your blood all day and all night to every part of your body. Your brain, lungs, skin and muscles need blood to keep them working properly.

A doctor uses a stethoscope to listen to your heart pumping in your chest.

Your heart doesn't work as hard when you are asleep. When you wake up and start moving it beats faster.

Heartbeat

Your heart is hollow, which means it has empty space inside it. The space fills up with blood, then your heart muscles squeeze and push the blood out again. Your heart beats every time your heart muscles squeeze tight.

Activity

Fill a balloon with water. Your heart fills up with blood like this. Gently squeeze the balloon with your hand. This is like your heart muscles squeezing. Watch the water squirt out. Blood spurts out of your heart and into your blood vessels in the same way.

Be careful where you squirt the water!

There are two sides of your heart, the left side and the right side. Each side has two rooms or chambers. The right side of your heart pumps blood into your lungs to collect **oxygen**. The left side of your heart pumps blood into your body.

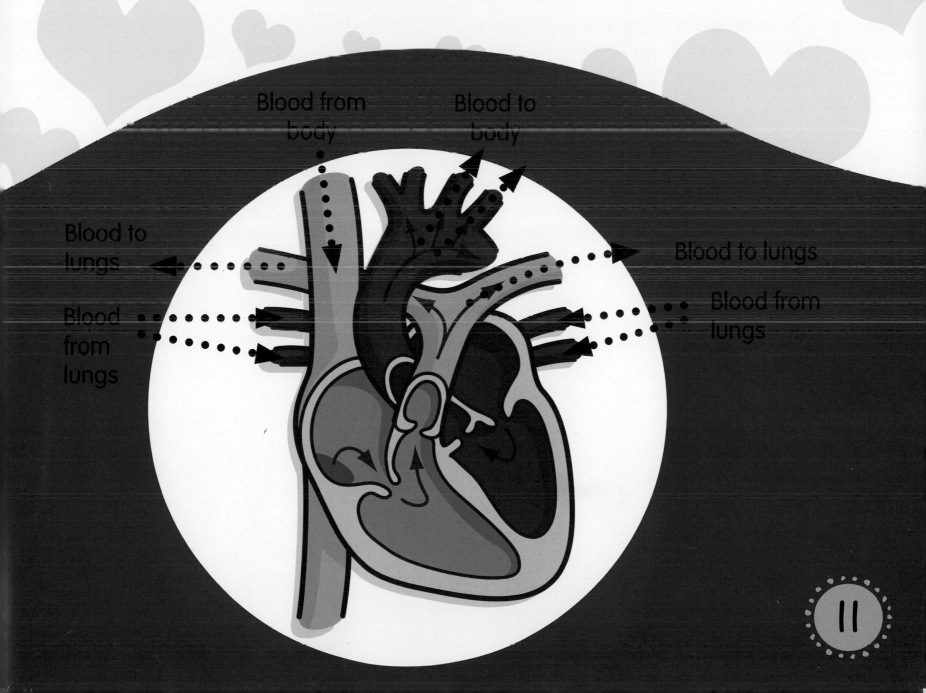

Blood from body

Blood to body

Blood to lungs

Blood to lungs

Blood from lungs

Blood from lungs

Veins and arteries

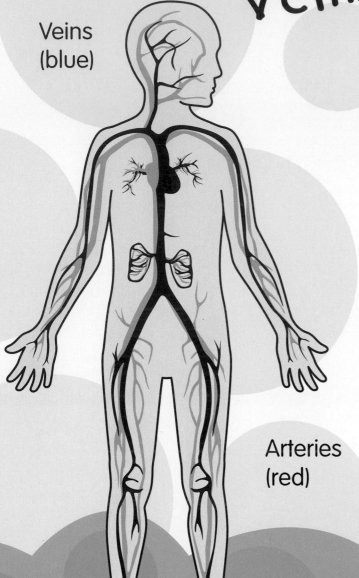

Veins
(blue)

Arteries
(red)

Your heart pumps your blood into tubes called **blood vessels**. Blood vessels called arteries carry blood away from your heart to every other part of your body. Blood vessels called veins bring blood back to your heart.

When you exercise, your body warms up and sometimes your skin turns red. This is because blood rushes to the blood vessels in your skin to keep you cool.

Around and around

Your blood is always moving around your body and through your heart. This movement is called circulation. It takes less than a minute for your heart to pump blood to every part of your body!

Activity

You can see blood flowing through your hand. Hold your right hand in the air for a few moments. Hang your left hand down by your side. Now look at the color of each hand. It is harder for your heart to pump blood upward, so your right hand looks pale because there is less blood in it. It is easy for blood to flow downward, so your left hand is red because it is full of blood.

Blood

Your blood is like a delivery truck. It carries oxygen from your lungs and nutrients from your food to every part of your body.

Your blood is full of tiny cells, which carry the oxygen. These cells give your blood its red color.

If you fall and cut yourself, your blood dries into a hard scab and your skin heals underneath the scab.

Feel the beat

When you are working hard, if you are running for example, your body needs more oxygen from your blood, so your heart beats faster.

You can feel your heartbeat in the blood vessels on your wrists. This is called your pulse.

Activity

Feel your pulse. Now run on the spot for a few moments. Feel your pulse again.

Your heart usually beats about 90 times a minute.

Your pulse gets faster when you work hard.

Lungs

Your lungs are the part of your body you **breathe** with. They are like two big sacks in your chest. Your left lung is a bit smaller than your right lung to make room for your heart. Your lungs are protected by your ribs.

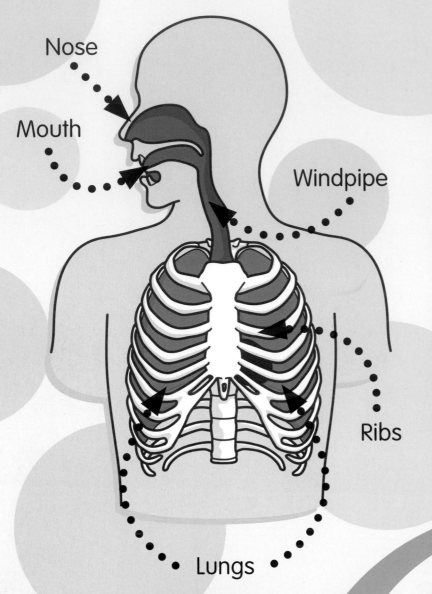

Nose

Mouth

Windpipe

Ribs

Lungs

The insides of your lungs are like sponges. They soak up air instead of water.

Ribs

Lung muscle that squeezes air in and out

Spongy inside of lung

Oxygen is a gas in the air. Your body needs oxygen from the air to stay alive, so you need to breathe air in and out of your lungs all the time.

Humans can't breathe under water, unless they use a tube called a snorkel while swimming.

Breathing in

You breathe air in through your mouth and nose. Air goes down your **windpipe** into your lungs. As your lungs fill up, they get bigger.

Tiny hairs in your nose and windpipe catch bits of dirt and help to clean the air going into your lungs.

Activity

You can feel your lungs fill with air. Put your hands on your ribs. Breathe in deeply. Feel your ribs lift and your chest get bigger as your lungs fill with air.

Oxygen from the air goes into tiny blood vessels called capillaries in your lungs. Blood full of oxygen flows to your heart and your heart pumps it all around your body.

When you work hard, your heart and lungs work hard too, and give you the extra oxygen that your body needs.

Breathing out

When you breathe in, fresh air goes into your lungs. After your lungs have taken oxygen from the air, you breathe it out. The stale air goes up your windpipe and out through your mouth and nose.

The air you breathe out gets warm as it goes through your body.

Activity

20

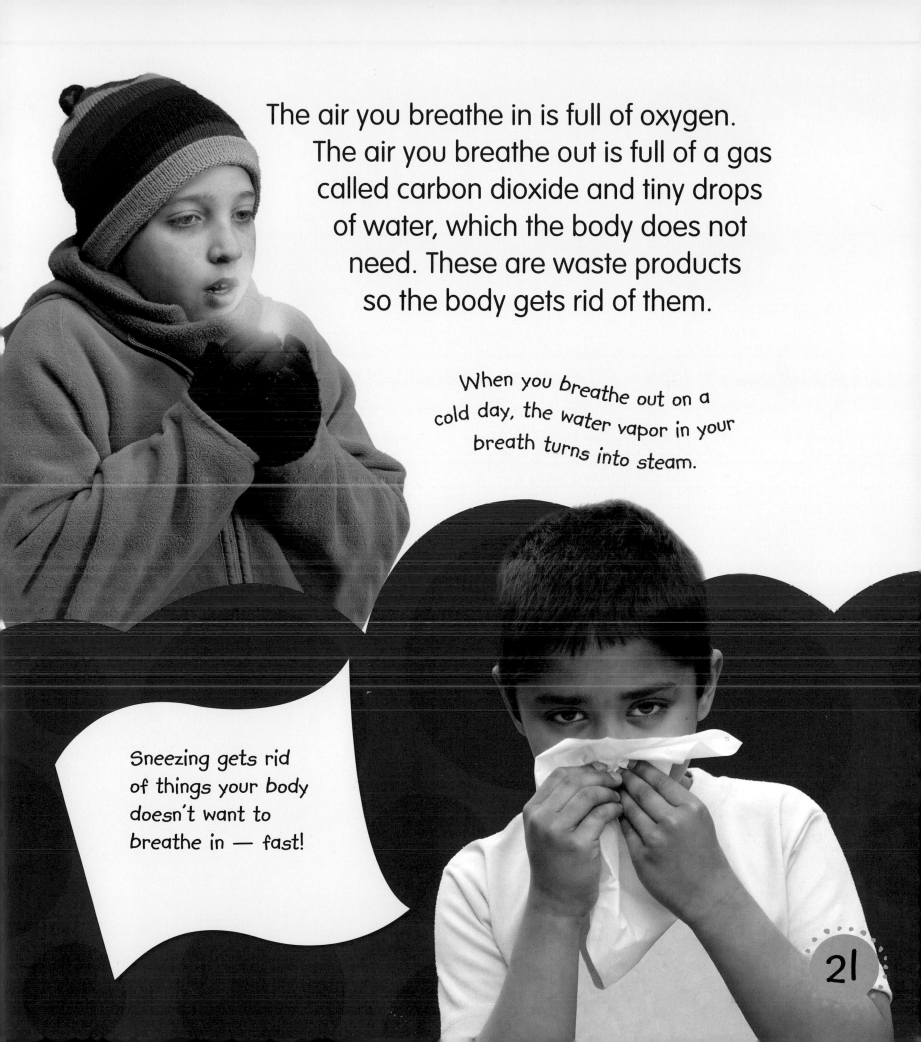

The air you breathe in is full of oxygen. The air you breathe out is full of a gas called carbon dioxide and tiny drops of water, which the body does not need. These are waste products so the body gets rid of them.

When you breathe out on a cold day, the water vapor in your breath turns into steam.

Sneezing gets rid of things your body doesn't want to breathe in — fast!

21

Blah Blah Blah Blah

Blah Blah

Talking

You need your lungs to breathe and to talk. You speak and sing with the small lump you can see and feel in your throat called your voice box, or larynx.

Activity

Feel your voice box. Make all kinds of different sounds — shout, screech and whisper. Does your voice box move when you make a sound?

22

You make sounds when air goes over folds of muscle called vocal cords in your voice box. The more air that goes over the folds, the louder the sounds!

Shouting uses lots of air. When you shout, you soon get out of breath!

Hiccupping happens when air rushes in and hits your voice box in a funny way.

23

Healthy heart and lungs

Look after your heart and lungs. Keeping active makes your heart and lungs work harder. Hard work makes them strong and healthy so they can help to keep your whole body healthy.

Healthy eating

You can help protect your heart, blood vessels and lungs by eating fresh food, lots of fruit and vegetables and not too much fat, salt or sugar.

Healthy food is good for you and delicious, too!

24

Fresh air

Fresh air is good for your lungs. Sometimes the air in big cities is polluted by fumes from cars. Polluted air is bad for you because it contains tiny bits of smoke and dust that enter your lungs and make you cough.

Take a trip to the countryside or to the seaside where the air is fresh and clean.

Sleep

When you are asleep your brain makes sure you keep breathing in and out during the night without having to think about it.

When you wake up after a good night's sleep, you are rested and ready for a busy day.

Stamina

Exercises that make you breathe faster help your heart and lungs to work better. The better they work, the longer you can keep going. This is called **stamina**.

This person has plenty of stamina. He can keep dancing without getting out of breath.

Your heart is a kind of muscle. Exercise makes it stronger. Exercises that make you breathe faster are called aerobic exercises. Running, swimming and dancing are different sorts of aerobic exercise.

Swimming is one kind of aerobic exercise.

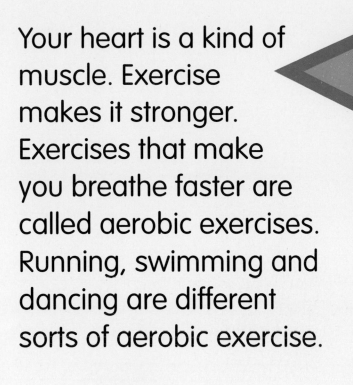

Activity

Run on the spot, lifting your knees as high as you can. Keep going for as long as you can. Doing this every day will increase your stamina.

27

Warming up

You need to warm up your muscles before you do any energetic exercise. You can warm up by walking and then running gently.

This soccer team is warming up their muscles by stretching.

These runners are stretching the tendons in their legs to warm up before a race.

28

The more you exercise, the fitter you become, but you should gradually increase the amount of exercise you do. A little bit more exercise each day will make your muscles stronger and increase your stamina.

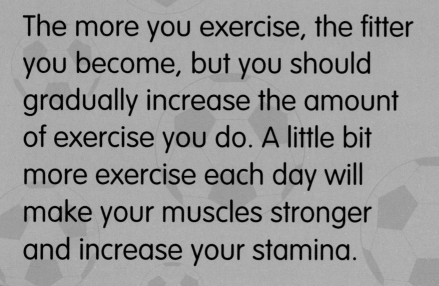

Activity

Try these warming-up exercises.

1. Stand on one leg and bend the other foot back to touch your bottom.

2. Keeping your legs straight, touch one foot and then the other foot.

Cooling down

It is important to allow your body to cool down gently after exercise. Cooling-down exercises help your muscles, heart and lungs to slow down before resting.

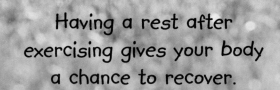

Having a rest after exercising gives your body a chance to recover.

Exercise can make you hot
and sweaty. If the air is cold,
put on a sweatshirt, so that
you do not cool down too fast.

Running around and sweating
often makes you thirsty, so
have a drink afterward.

Activity

Marching on the spot is a
good cooling-down activity.
March slower and slower,
and then stop.

Notes for parents and teachers

1. Point to the position of your heart, just to the left and middle of your chest. Make a fist to show the size of your heart. An adult's fist is bigger than a child's fist. Talk about the comparative size of a child's heart and an adult's heart.

2. Feel your ribs and breastbone. Discuss how your ribs protect your heart. Explain that your heart needs to be protected because it is soft. Use the word "muscle" and feel other muscles that let you move. Use the word "pump" and talk about how a pump pushes liquid.

3. Talk about how blood travels through blood vessels in the same way that water travels through pipes. Find pipes around the home. Talk about what happens to water without pipes to travel through!

4. Find the blood vessels in your wrist. Feel each other's pulse and explain that each beat is your heart pumping blood all around your body.

5. Breathe in and out through your nose and mouth. Try putting your hand in front of your face. Feel air coming out of your nose. Now feel it coming out of your mouth. Does air come out of both your nose and your mouth at the same time?

6. Run together on the spot and feel how your heart beats faster and you breathe more quickly after exercise. Explain that this is because your body needs more oxygen when you work hard. Feel your heart beat and notice that your breathing slows down when you rest.

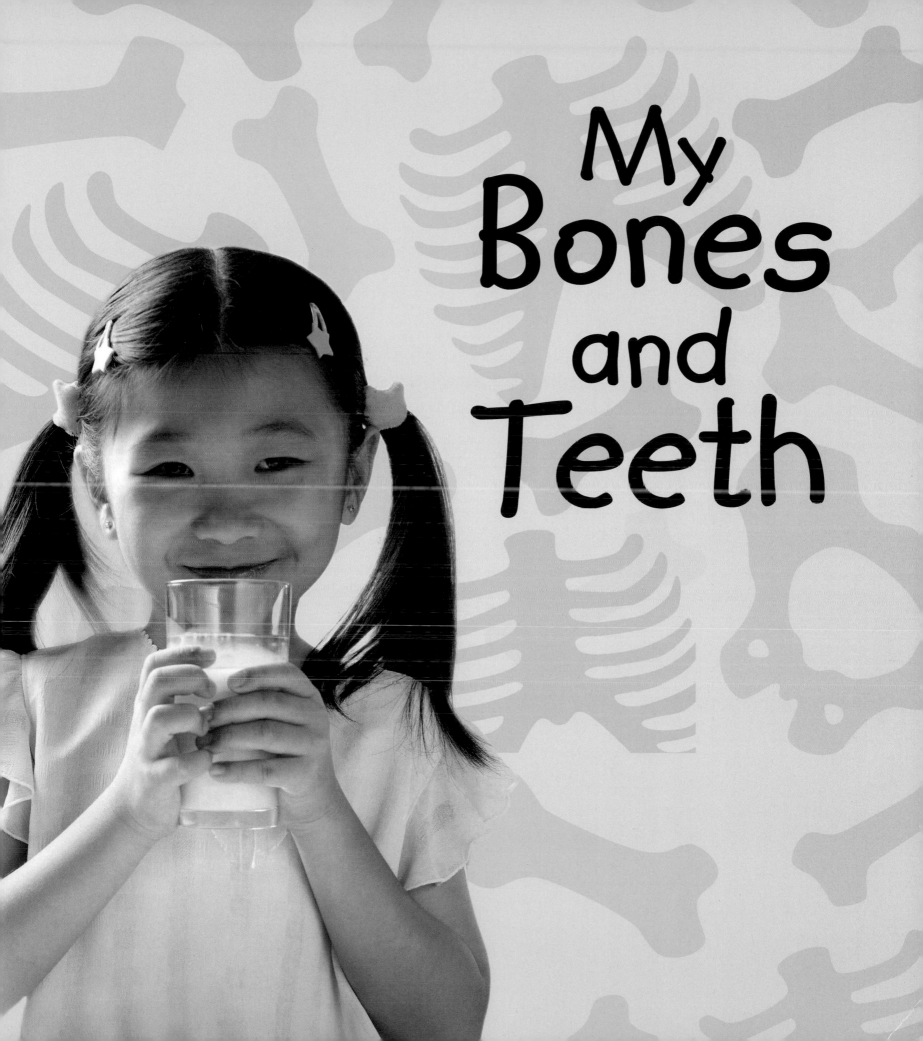

My Bones and Teeth

What is your skeleton?

Your skeleton is like a strong frame. It gives your body its **shape**, holds you upright and lets you move. It **protects** soft parts of your body, such as your heart and lungs.

Your skeleton is made up of bones of different shapes and sizes. Each bone has a job to do.

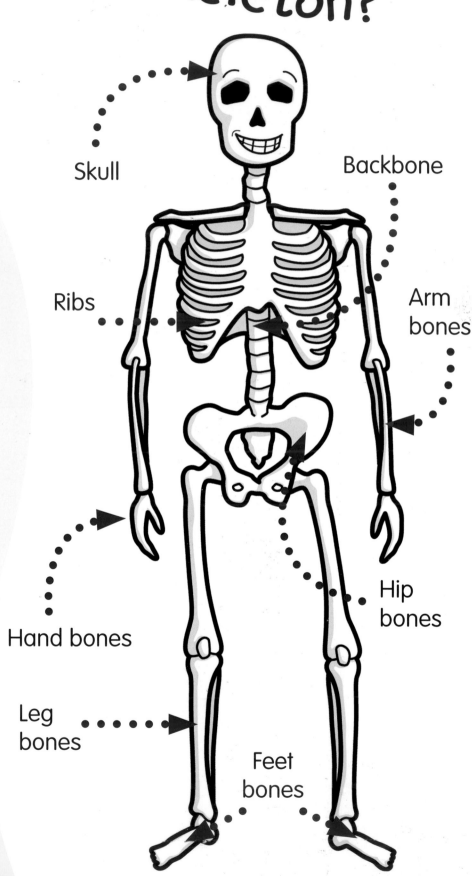

Skull

Backbone

Ribs

Arm bones

Hand bones

Hip bones

Leg bones

Feet bones

Your body is alive and growing, and so are your bones. As you grow older, your bones become harder and stronger. By the time you are fully grown, you will have 206 bones.

A baby has tiny hands and feet and soft, bendy bones.

Activity

Which of your bones can you feel through your skin?

Can you feel the top of the bone in your upper arm? Your ribs?

35

Healthy exercise

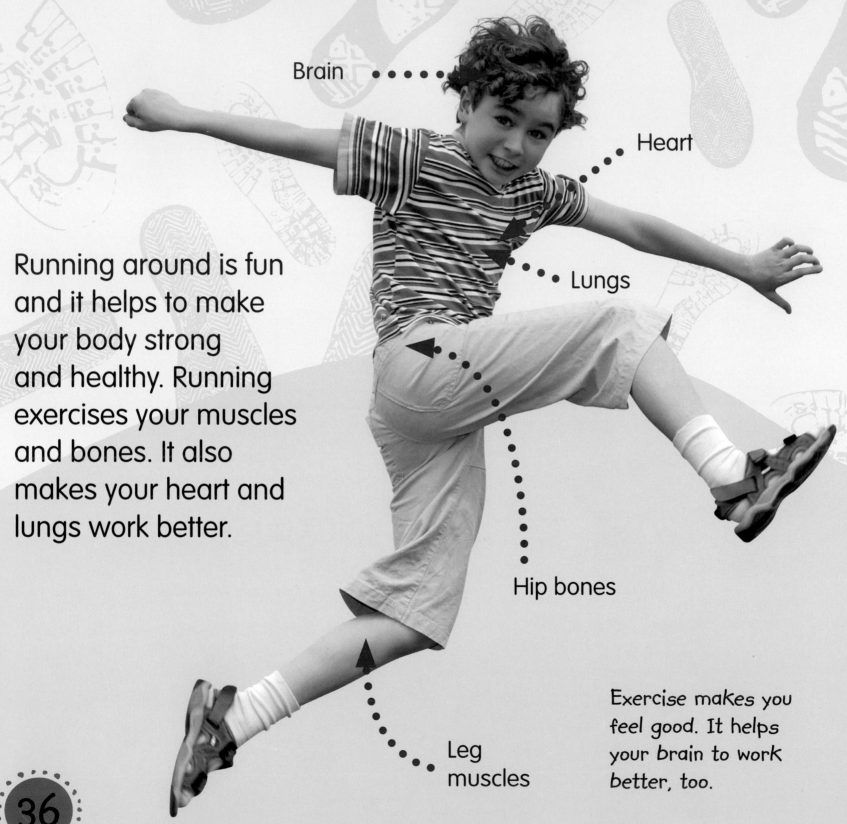

Brain

Heart

Lungs

Running around is fun and it helps to make your body strong and healthy. Running exercises your muscles and bones. It also makes your heart and lungs work better.

Hip bones

Leg muscles

Exercise makes you feel good. It helps your brain to work better, too.

36

Climbing and swinging are both fun. They are also a good way to exercise.

Running is one kind of exercise. There are many others, including swimming and cycling.

Walking is good exercise, too. Walking to school is healthier than going by car.

37

Stronger muscles

You use your muscles to move. Muscles move your bones so that you can move the different parts of your body. The more you exercise, the stronger your muscles become.

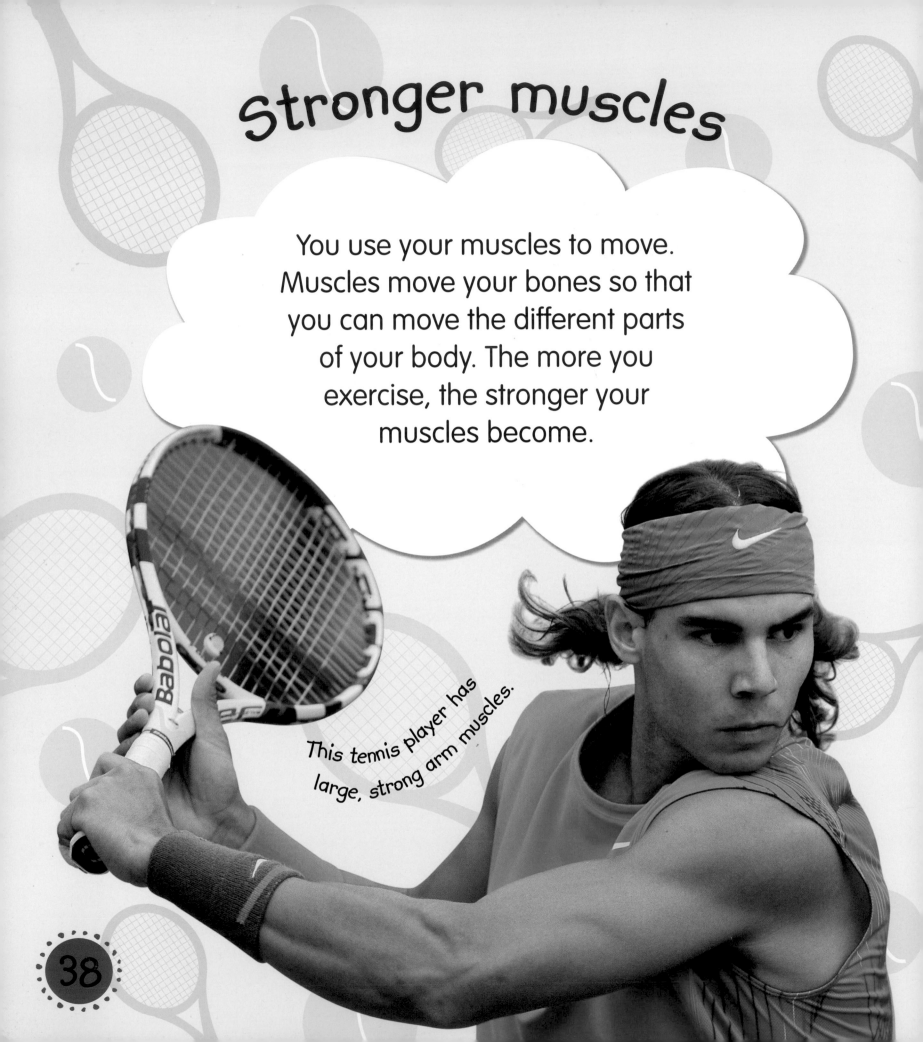

This tennis player has large, strong arm muscles.

Muscles are made of bundles of strings, called muscle fibers. Exercising a muscle makes the fibers thicker and stronger. This makes your muscle bigger.

All muscles in your body, including arm muscles, are made of fibers.

Muscle fibers

Activity

Feel your muscles. Sit on the floor with your legs bent in front of you. Hold the back of your legs, then straighten them. Can you feel the leg muscles tightening?

39

Your bones

Your bones need to be strong and light. Bones are light enough to let you jump, and strong enough not to break when you land.

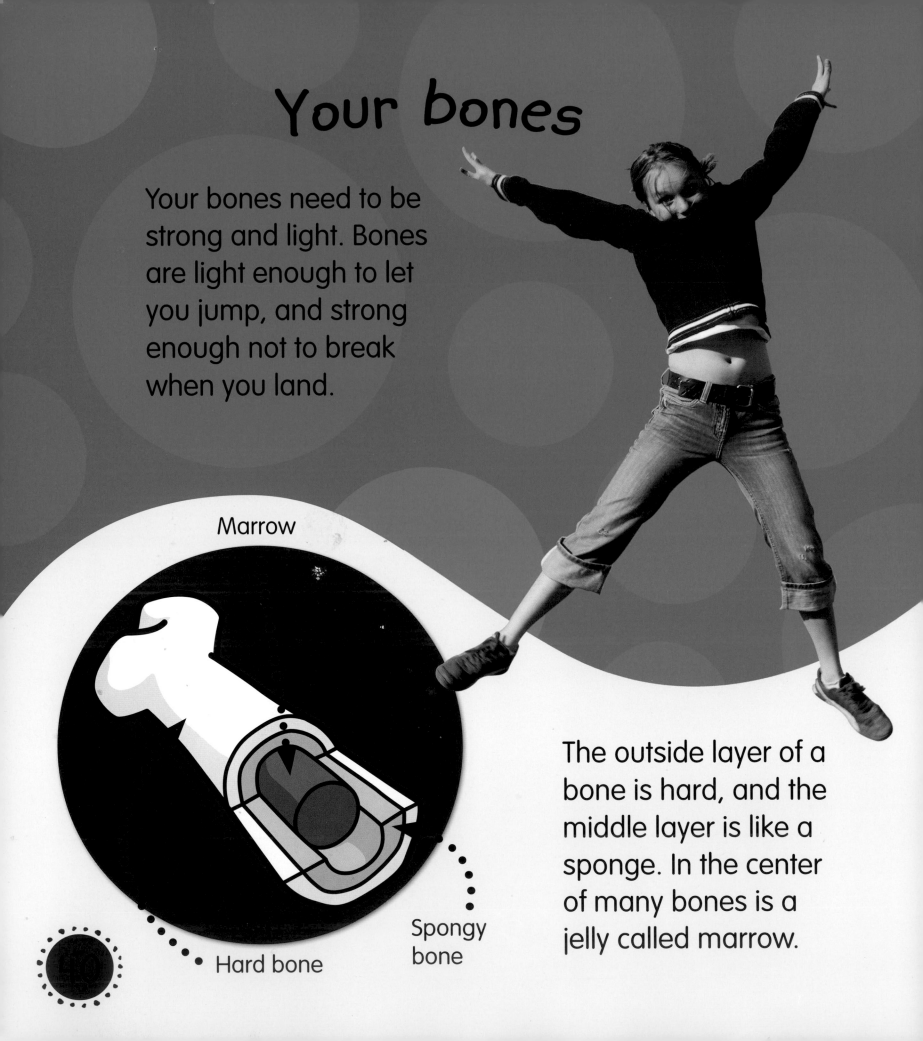

Marrow

Hard bone

Spongy bone

The outside layer of a bone is hard, and the middle layer is like a sponge. In the center of many bones is a jelly called marrow.

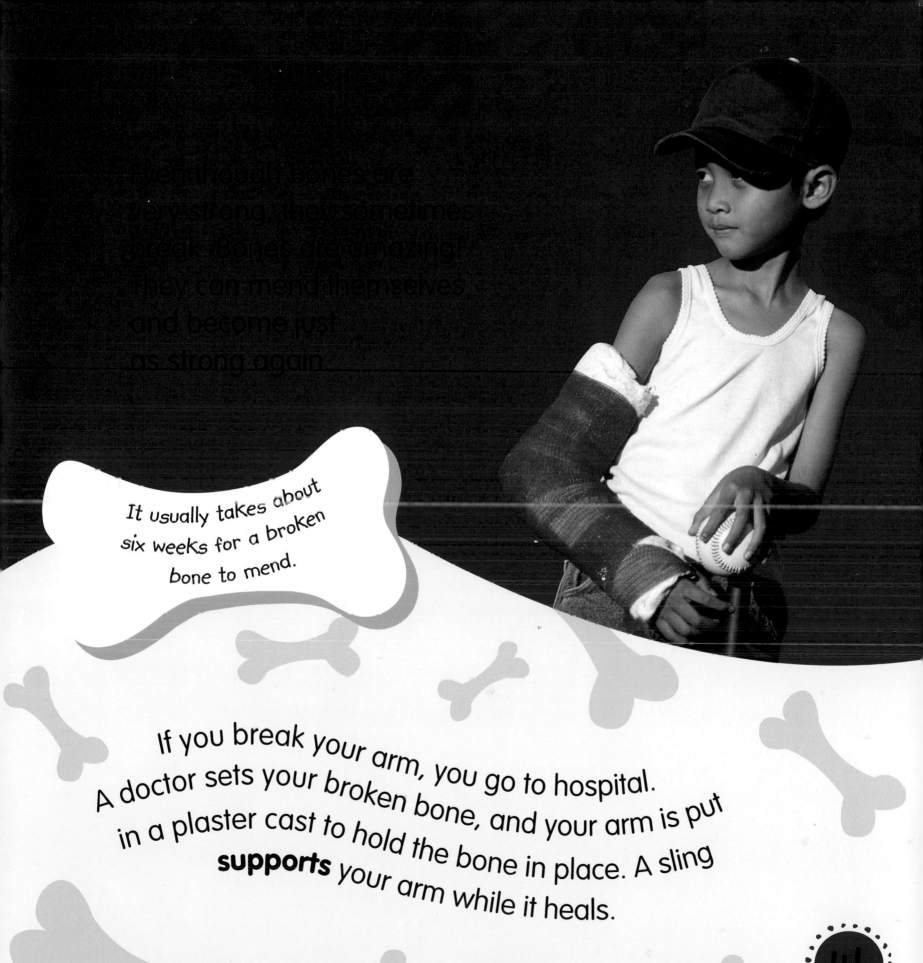

Even though bones are
very strong, they sometimes
break. Bones are amazing!
They can mend themselves
and become just
as strong again.

It usually takes about
six weeks for a broken
bone to mend.

If you break your arm, you go to hospital.
A doctor sets your broken bone, and your arm is put
in a plaster cast to hold the bone in place. A sling
supports your arm while it heals.

41

Whatever exercise you enjoy, such as running, dancing or ball games, will keep you active and help your bones to grow strong.

Do something active every day.

Wear a helmet when you ride a bicycle to protect your skull. Wear pads to protect your knees and elbows when you skate.

You can have fun and look after your bones!

Joints

Your bones join together at places called **joints**. Most of the joints in your skeleton can move.

If you didn't have joints, you would be as stiff as a statue.

Activity

Move around.
Can you work out which of
your joints move?
What kind of movements
can they make?

Your joints move in different ways. You have "ball-and-socket" joints, where your arms join your shoulders and where your legs join your hips. These joints let your arms and legs move round in a circle.

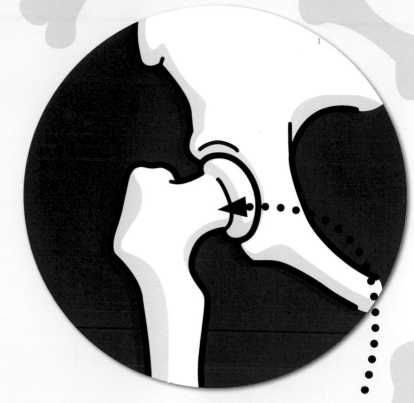

Ball-and-socket joint

Elbows and knees are "hinge" joints. They move backward and forward like the hinges on a door.

Your skull

Your skull is made up of several bones. It is very strong. Its most important job is to protect your brain. Feel the shape of your skull. It has two holes for your eyes. Your jaw opens and closes when you talk and also when you eat.

The top of your skull is exactly the right shape and size to cover and protect your brain.

46

The bones in your skull give your face its shape. We all have a forehead, eyes, nose, a mouth and a chin. Everyone looks just a bit different so we can recognize each other easily.

It would be very confusing if we all looked exactly the same.

Activity

Look in the mirror and draw a picture of your face. Then, draw your friend's face. Which parts of the drawings look the same and which look different?

Your backbone

Spine

Your backbone, or "spine," runs right down the middle of your back. It is made up of 26 small bones. If it were made of just one long bone, you would not be able to bend or twist.

Activity

Bend your knees, curl your back, touch your toes and then stand up again. Feel your backbone bend and straighten up again.

Your backbone holds you upright. If you stand, walk and sit with a straight back, your spine supports your whole body. If you let your back bend while you are standing or sitting, you will soon start to ache all over.

Gymnasts hold their back straight to help them balance.

Your ribs

Your ribs are shaped like a cage. They protect your heart, which pumps blood around your body, and your lungs, which you use for breathing.

You have 12 pairs of ribs. They are fixed to your backbone. The top seven pairs of ribs are fixed to your breastbone at the front.

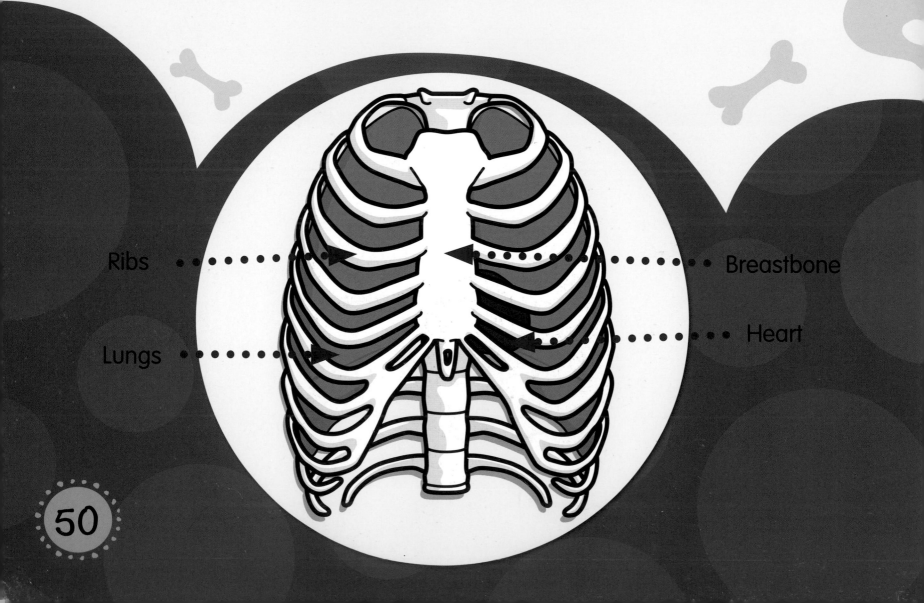

Ribs

Lungs

Breastbone

Heart

You can feel your ribs and you can probably see the shape of them through your skin, too.
The bottom two pairs of ribs are only fixed at the back so they can move more easily when you breathe in and out.

Activity

Take a deep breath. Your lungs will fill up with air just like this balloon.

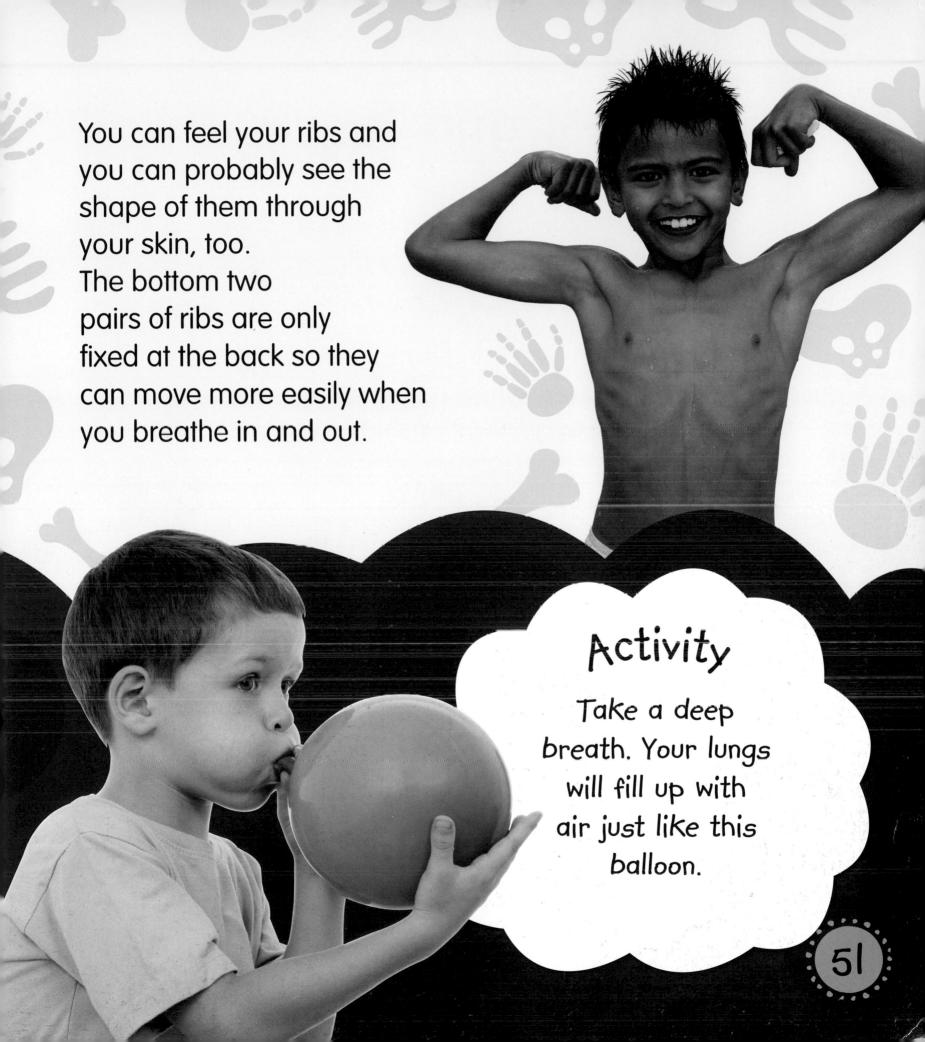

Arms and hands

You use your arms and hands to grip and to pick things up, write, draw and play with toys!

Each arm, wrist and hand is made up of 30 bones, which help you make all these different movements.

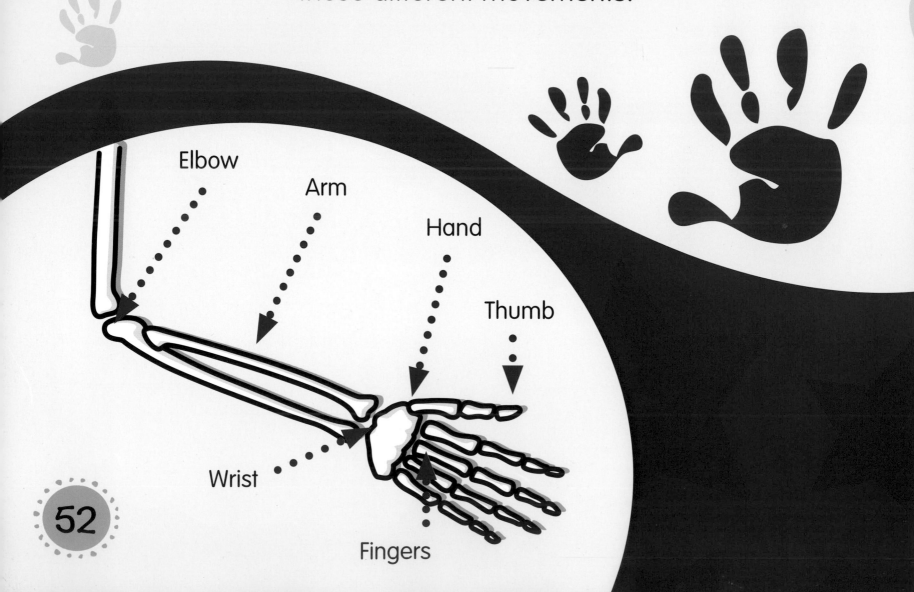

Elbow

Arm

Hand

Thumb

Wrist

Fingers

The bone in the top of your arm is strong and thick. You have two thinner bones in the bottom of your arm and 27 bones in your hand and wrist!

Lots of little bones in your fingers help you make small movements.

Activity

Make a model with modeling clay. Notice how you move all the bones in your arms and hands.

53

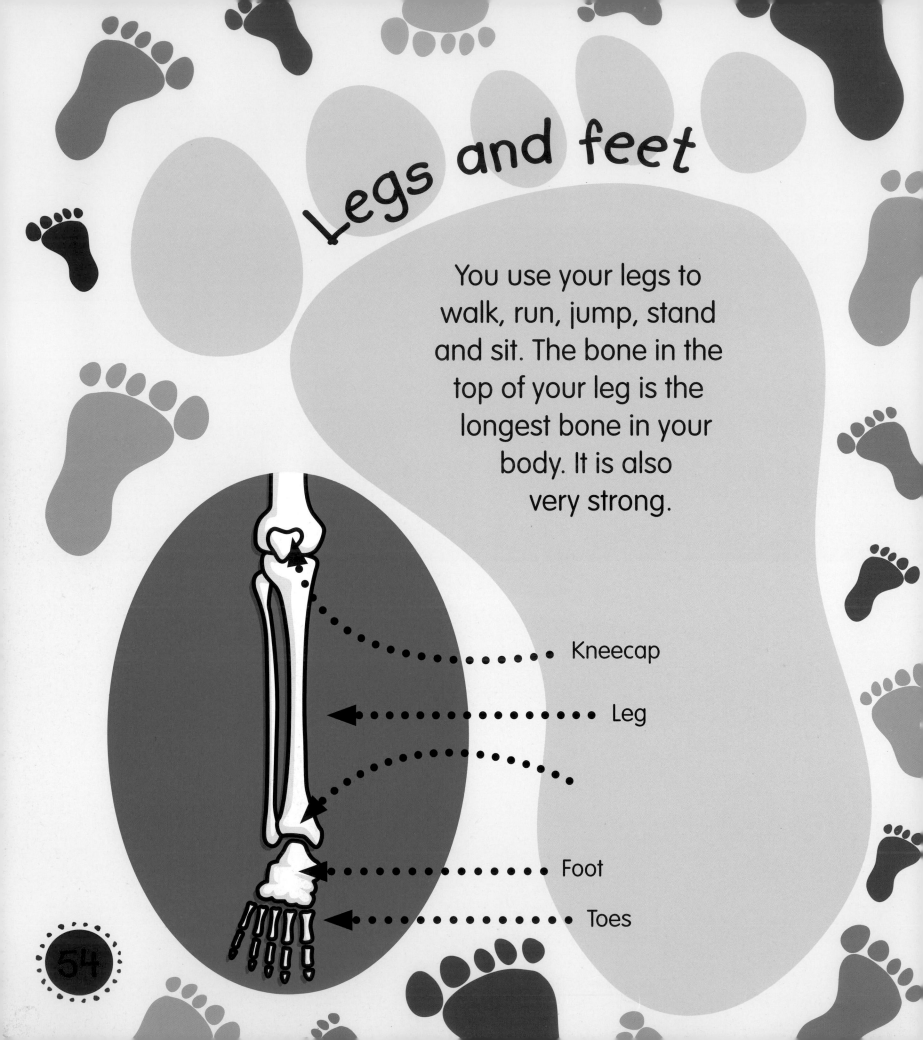

Legs and feet

You use your legs to walk, run, jump, stand and sit. The bone in the top of your leg is the longest bone in your body. It is also very strong.

Kneecap

Leg

Foot

Toes

54

A bone called the kneecap protects your knee joint. Children often cut and bruise their knees, so kneecaps have an important job to do!

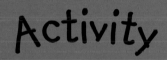

Have you ever cut or bruised your knee?

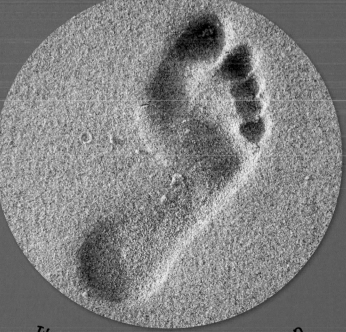

It is fun to make footprints on a sandy beach. You can make footprints at home, too!

Activity

Put some dark paper in a tray and sprinkle flour on top of it. Stand in the flour. Now carefully step out without smudging the flour. Can you see how the bones in your foot spread out to help you stand?

Healthy teeth

Your teeth are very important. You need strong teeth to bite into your food and chew it so that it is easy to swallow. You have to brush your teeth regularly to keep them clean and strong.

You also use your teeth when you speak, especially your front teeth. For example, try to say the word "teeth" without touching your front teeth with your tongue.

Your teeth help you to make "hard" sounds such as "t" and "d."

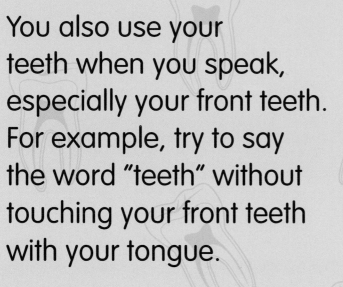

Activity

Use a mirror to check your teeth. How many do you have? Do you have any gaps?

Different shapes of teeth

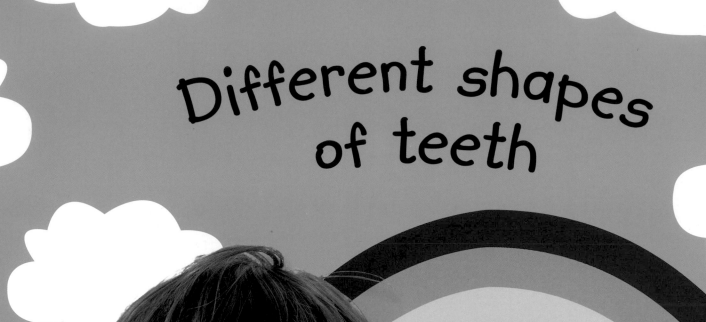

You have three kinds of teeth. The front teeth have a wide, sharp edge, and are called incisors. You use them like a knife to slice through food.

Your front teeth are sharp and strong.

58

Behind your front teeth are four sharp canine teeth. You use your canine teeth to tear off mouthfuls of food.

The teeth at the back of your mouth are called molars. You use them for chewing.

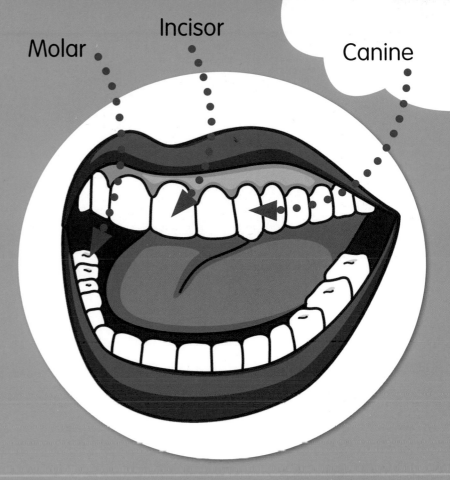

Molar
Incisor
Canine

Teeth have different shapes so you can bite and chew food.

Activity

Put a piece of cracker between two spoons. Crush the cracker between the spoons. This is how your molars grind up food.

Two sets of teeth

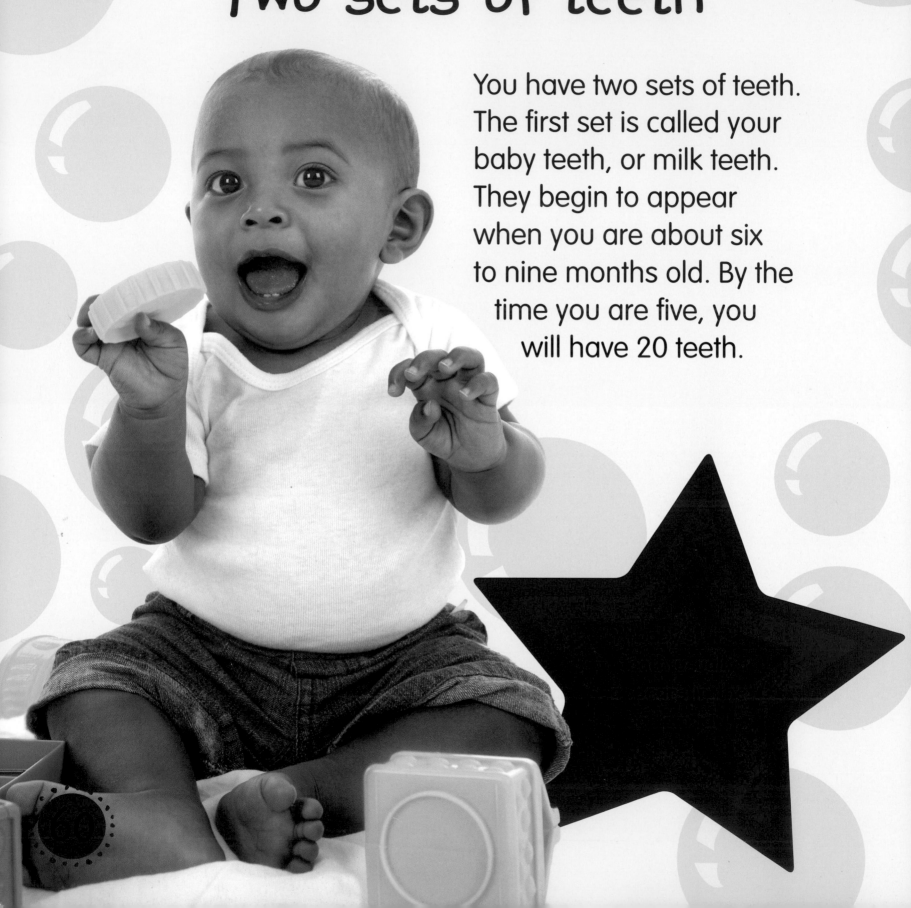

You have two sets of teeth. The first set is called your baby teeth, or milk teeth. They begin to appear when you are about six to nine months old. By the time you are five, you will have 20 teeth.

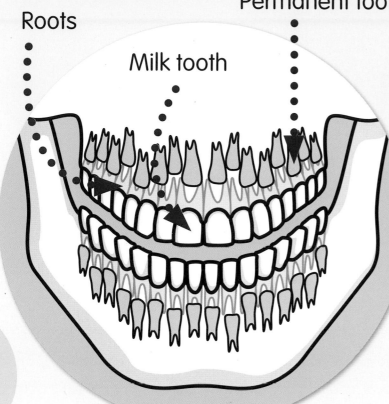

Roots

Permanent tooth

Milk tooth

Each milk tooth has a permanent tooth growing below it.

The second set of teeth grow below the milk teeth. They are called permanent or adult teeth, and there are 32 of them.

As each permanent tooth grows bigger, it pushes the milk tooth above it. This loosens the milk tooth until it falls out.

Activity

When a milk tooth falls out, examine it closely. Can you see any root? Compare its size to an adult tooth.

Inside a tooth

A tooth has three layers. The outer layer of **enamel** is the hardest thing in your body. The **dentine** below is as strong as bone. The center is filled with soft **pulp** that contains blood vessels and nerves.

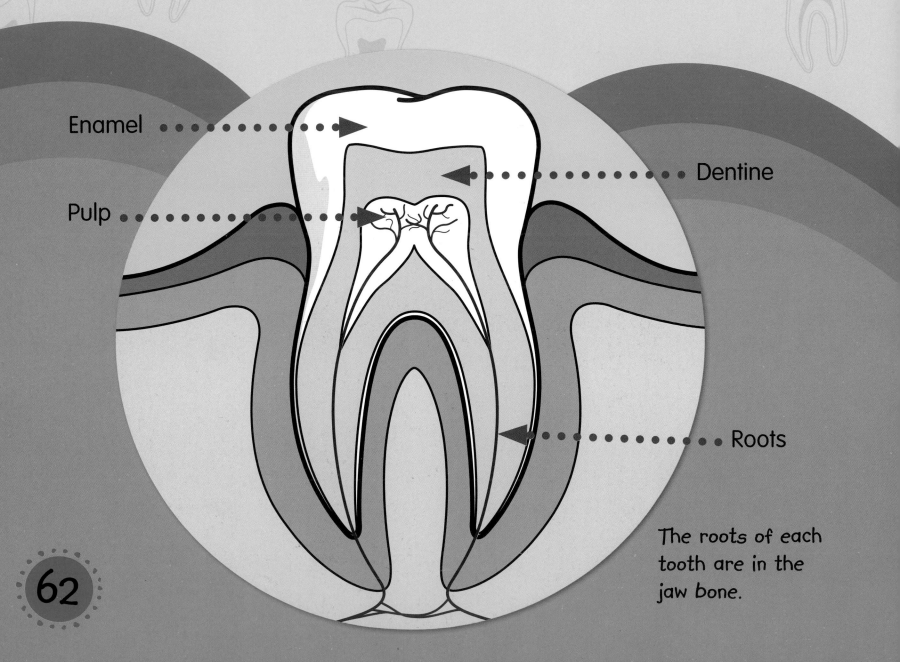

Enamel

Dentine

Pulp

Roots

The roots of each tooth are in the jaw bone.

Acid can damage your teeth by making a hole in the enamel. The hole is called **tooth decay**.

A small hole in a tooth is called a cavity.

Activity

Put a whole uncooked egg in a glass, cover it with vinegar, and leave it overnight. Vinegar is an acid. It takes the **calcium** out of the eggshell in the same way that acid in your mouth attacks your teeth. In the morning, the eggshell will be soft.

63

What causes tooth decay?

Your mouth contains germs called bacteria. They are too small to see, but they feed on sugar left in your mouth. As they feed, they make **plaque**.

Plaque contains acid, which can cause tooth decay. Plaque and bacteria can also affect your gums. They may make your gums bleed.

When tooth decay causes a hole or cavity, it can be very painful. Children and adults can suffer from tooth decay.

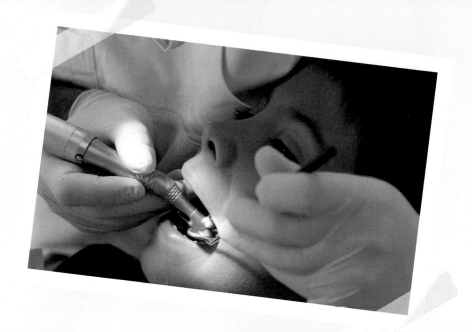

Dentists can treat tooth decay. They drill away the rotten part of the tooth and fill the hole. This is called a filling.

When a dentist fills a tooth, it stops decaying.

Activity

Find a large potato with one or more "eyes" in it. With adult help, dig out the eyes with a potato peeler. Put a teaspoon of icing sugar into a bowl and add two drops of water. Use the mixture to fill the holes, like a dentist fills teeth.

cleaning your teeth

Cleaning your teeth brushes away sugar and plaque. You should clean your teeth when you get up and before you go to bed. If possible, you should also clean them after meals.

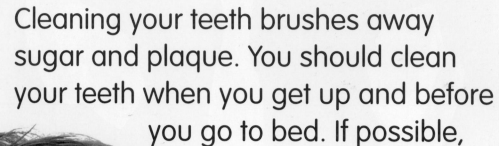

Try to clean your teeth after eating anything sweet.

Activity

Disclosing tablets show how well you have brushed your teeth. When you suck one, it colors the plaque red or purple. Clean your teeth again until all the color has gone.

Always brush from your gums to the tips of your teeth. Brush the back of each tooth as well as the front, and remember to clean the tops of your molars, as well as your gums.

67

Sugar damages your teeth

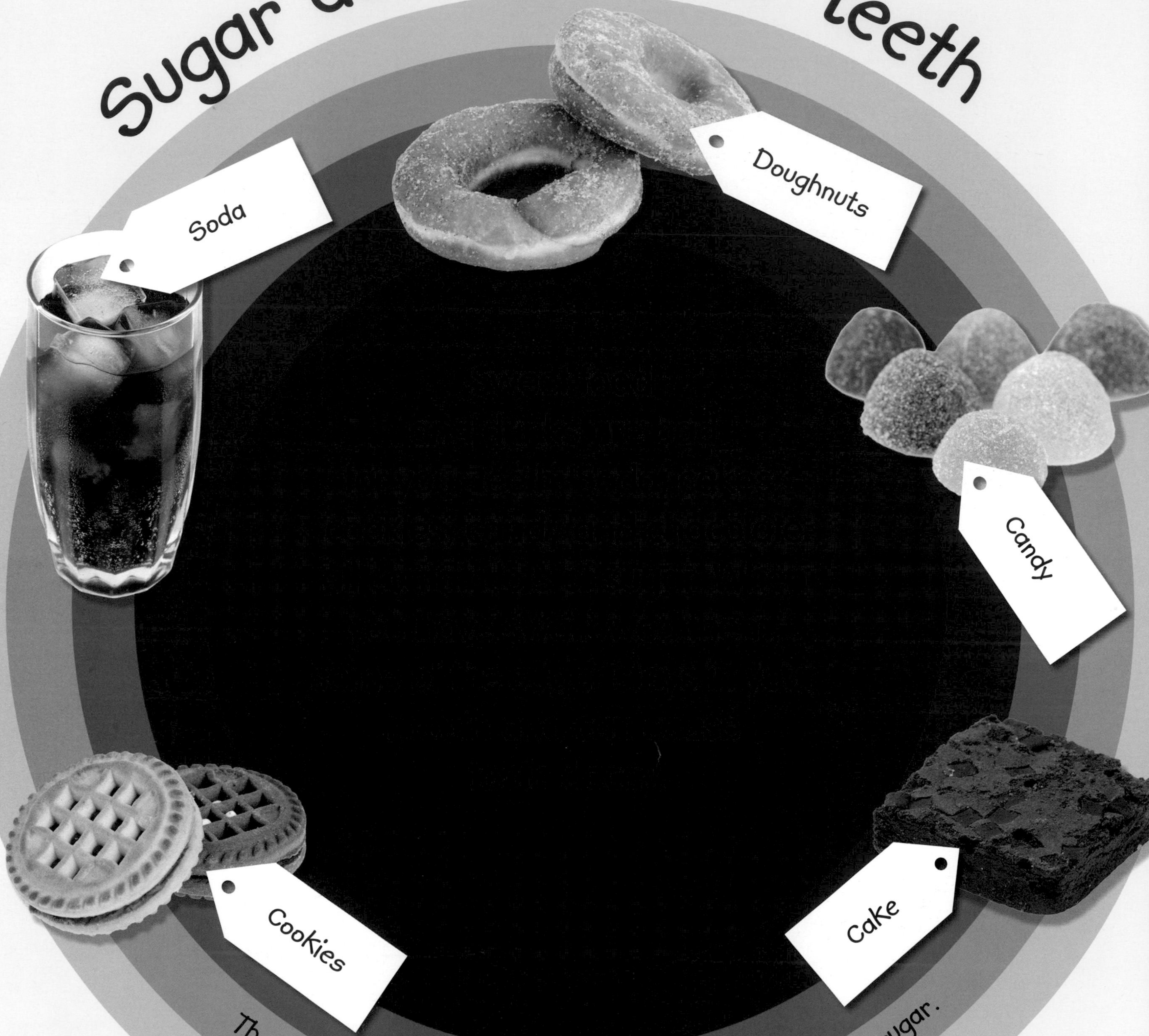

Soda

Doughnuts

Candy

Cake

Cookies

These are just some of the foods and drinks that contain sugar.

Have a drink of water after eating or drinking something sweet. The water will help to wash the sugar away. Even better, clean your teeth.

Drinking water helps to clean your teeth.

Activity

Wash your toothbrush well in clean water after you have used it. Examine it carefully to make sure all the bits of food have been washed away.

69

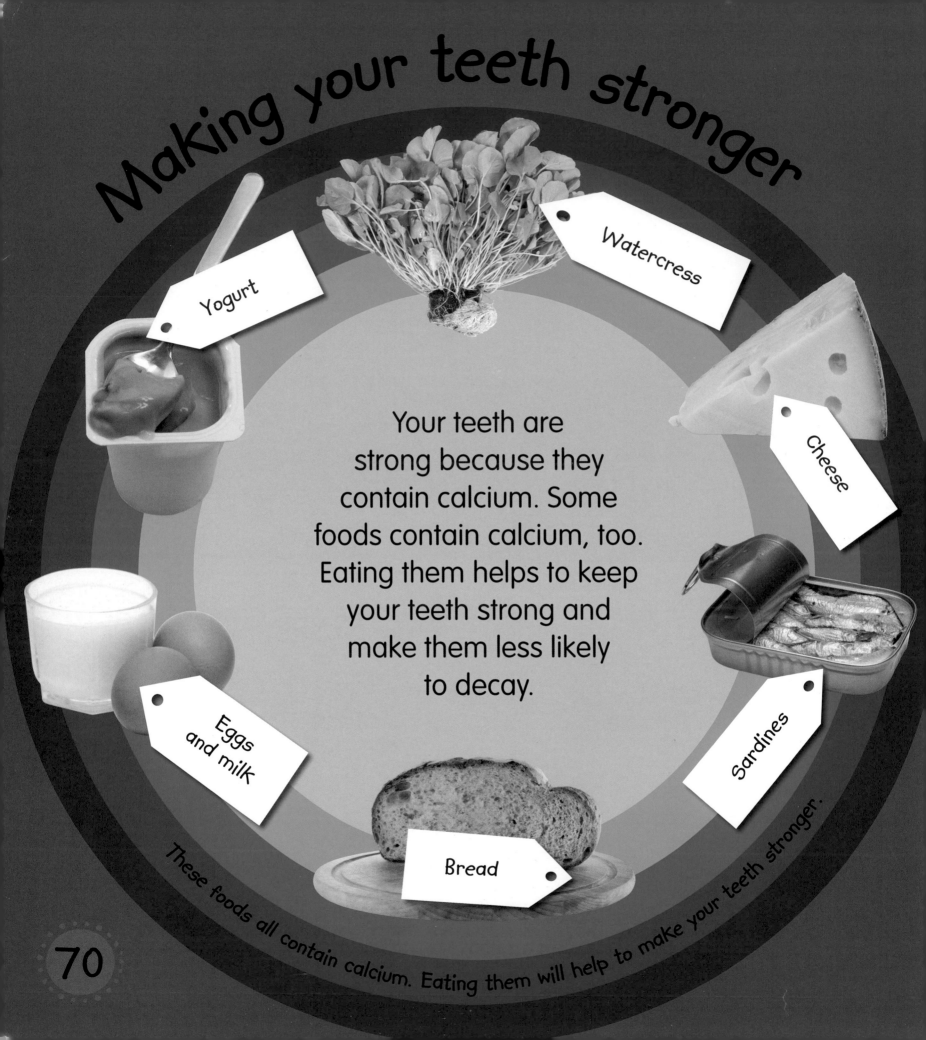

Making your teeth stronger

Watercress

Yogurt

Cheese

Your teeth are strong because they contain calcium. Some foods contain calcium, too. Eating them helps to keep your teeth strong and make them less likely to decay.

Sardines

Eggs and milk

Bread

These foods all contain calcium. Eating them will help to make your teeth stronger.

Fluoride makes the enamel on your teeth stronger. Most types of toothpaste contain fluoride, and, in some places, fluoride is also added to tap water.

Try not to swallow the toothpaste. If you often have too much fluoride, it can discolor your teeth.

Activity
Make a healthy, calcium-filled lunch. You could start with a cheese, ham and lettuce sandwich. Then you could eat a yogurt or an orange.

71

Going to the dentist

You should have a dental check-up every six months. The dentist looks at all your teeth to see if you have any tooth decay. The dentist also checks that your adult teeth are growing well.

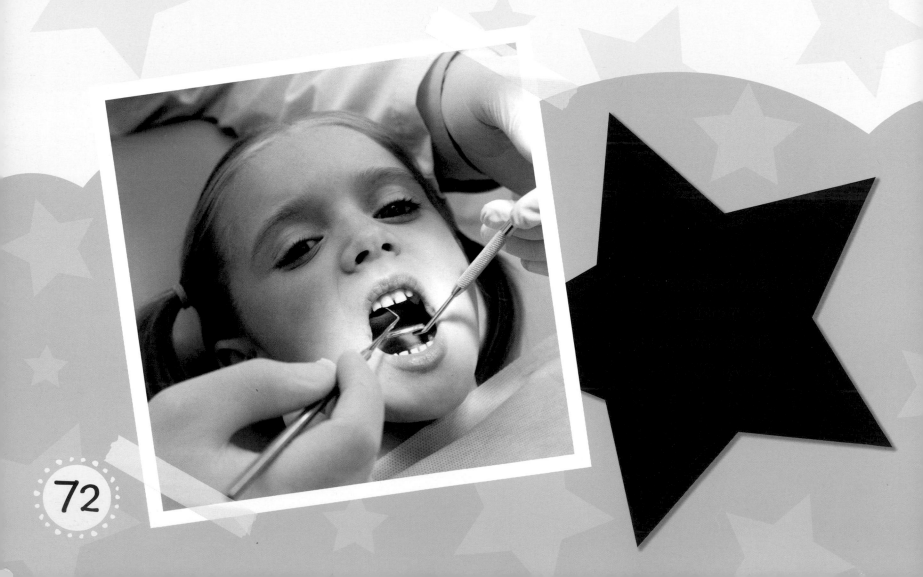

You may sometimes get toothache in one of your teeth. It might be caused by eating something very cold. If you have toothache that does not go away, you should go to the dentist.

Cold food can make your teeth hurt, but just for a moment.

New

Old

Activity
Check your toothbrush to make sure the bristles are straight and firm. If they are not, you need a new toothbrush.

73

Notes for parents and teachers

1. Have fun drawing a skeleton together. Talk about the shape of the bones you are drawing and feel them under your skin.

2. Visit a museum with skeletons on display or look at a book with pictures of human, animal or even dinosaur skeletons. Notice that they all have skulls and backbones. Discuss the differences in the shapes of the skeletons and the size of the bones.

3. Look at worms, slugs and snails, which do not have internal skeletons to support them. Notice how they move without bones and joints.

4. Find all the places in your body that bend and name the joints. You could play a game of "Simon says," changing the instructions to: "Simon says bend your elbow," (or wrist, knee, etc.). Sit down if you bend the wrong joint!

5. Talk to the children about how cleaning their teeth helps to prevent tooth decay.

6. Search the Internet to find diagrams of a full set of milk teeth and a full set of permanent teeth. Count the teeth and see which extra teeth are included in the permanent teeth.

7. Talk about tooth decay and the foods that contribute to it. Make a list of drinks and foods, particularly treats, that contain a lot of refined sugar. Discuss how you can limit the intake of these foods to once or twice a day, and how drinking water after having them or, better still, cleaning their teeth, helps to prevent tooth decay.

My Brain

What is your brain?

Your **brain** is inside your head.
You think with this part of your body.
Your brain controls everything you do.
While you are asleep, your brain
keeps on working.

Your dreams are what you are
thinking about in your sleep.

76

Your brain tells your body to
move. It tells you what you
see, smell, hear, taste and
touch. It even tells you if you
are happy or sad.

You learn new things
and remember them
using your brain.

77

Your brain

Your brain is kept safe inside a strong box of bone in your head called your **skull**. Your brain needs to be protected because it is soft.

Your skull is just the right size and shape for your brain to sit inside. Your skull is made up of two sets of bones. The bones of your face are in one set and the other set protects your brain.

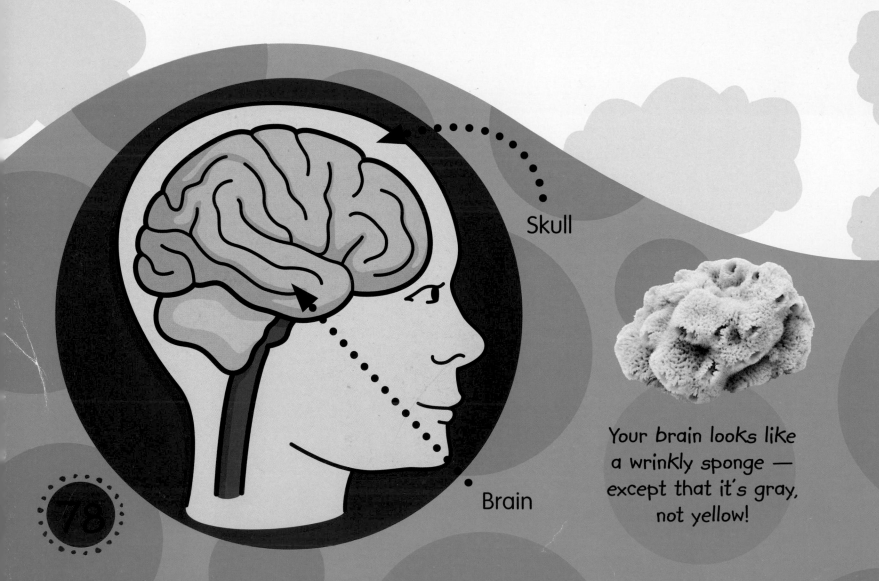

Skull

Brain

78

Your brain looks like a wrinkly sponge — except that it's gray, not yellow!

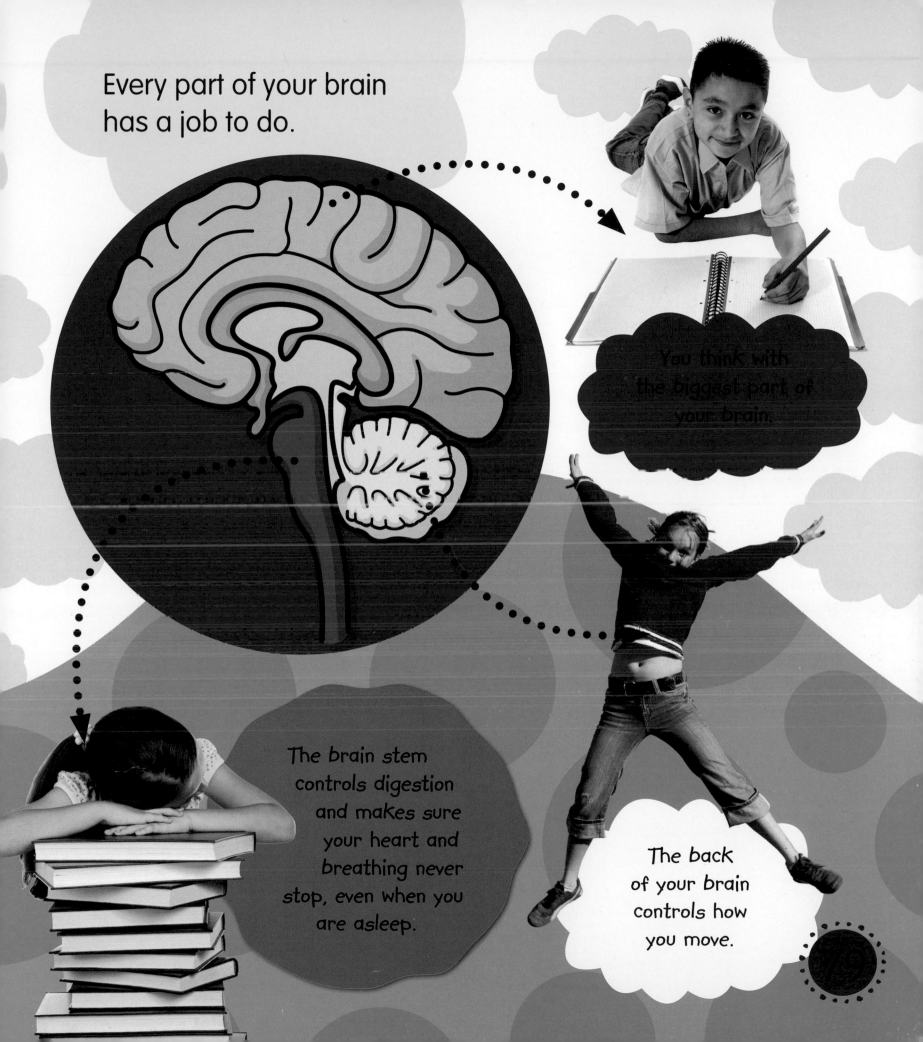

Every part of your brain has a job to do.

You think with the biggest part of your brain.

The brain stem controls digestion and makes sure your heart and breathing never stop, even when you are asleep.

The back of your brain controls how you move.

Nerves

Nerves carry **messages** from your brain to every part of your body and back again. Your nerves are like pathways. Messages run up and down them all the time.

Your spinal cord is a long tube of nerves down the middle of your back. The nerves in your spinal cord link your brain to every part of your body.

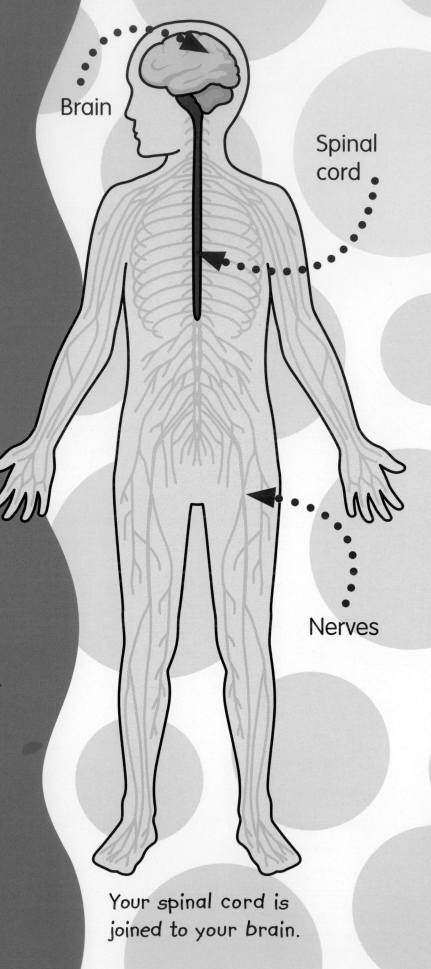

Brain

Spinal cord

Nerves

Your spinal cord is joined to your brain.

Two kinds of messages are sent along your nerves. One goes to your brain to tell it what is happening. The brain sends a reply to tell your body how to react.

This feels wet ...

Pull hand out of water to get dry.

Activity

Feel something soft, such as the fur of a cat. One message tells your brain "This feels soft." The reply message comes back. It tells your arm to move, pull your hand back, or to be gentle.

81

Senses

Your **senses** tell you what is going on around you. You have five senses.

You *see* with your eyes.
Your *hear* with your ears.
You *smell* with your nose.
Your *taste* with your tongue.
You *feel* with your skin.

Apple

When you see something, a message is sent along your nerves from your eyes to your brain.

Your brain tells you what you are seeing.

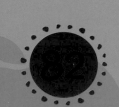

Your senses work together to tell you things.

Your eyes see flames, your nose smells smoke, your ears hear crackling and your brain tells you, "Fire!"

Your skin feels hot and warns you, "Don't touch!"

Activity

Can you tell what something is by only using one sense?

Smell an orange, soap, chocolate and a flower. Now feel them as well.

Does that help?

Quick as a flash!

You do some things as quick as a flash, without thinking about them! If your finger touches a hot mug, you get the message "hot" and quickly pull your finger away.

A flash of light makes you blink. Blinking protects your eyes from bright light!

84

Are you good at hitting a ball? Your brain tells you instantly where the ball is going so you can hit it.

Activity

With a friend, drop a pencil between each other's hands. Can you catch it? Whose brain sends messages the fastest?

85

Ball play

Many games involve throwing and catching balls. You need good **coordination** to do these sports well. Coordination involves using your eyes and brain to time your movements correctly.

Juggling needs good hand-and-eye coordination.

Your brain, eyes and muscles work together to help you head a ball.

86

Improve your ball skills! Keep a ball in the air. You can use any part of your body except your hands and arms. How many "keepie-uppies" can you do?

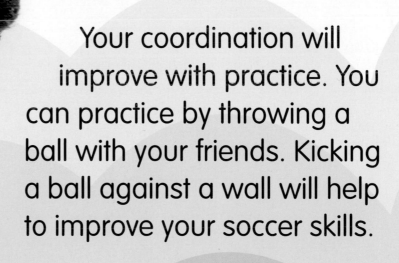

Your coordination will improve with practice. You can practice by throwing a ball with your friends. Kicking a ball against a wall will help to improve your soccer skills.

87

Memory

Your brain **remembers** things.
When you taste new food for the first
time, your brain remembers what it
looks like, how it tastes and smells
and if you like it.

When you
are given the food
again, your brain
remembers
whether you liked
it or not.

You can't remember everything, so your brain works out what is important and what is not so important.

What happened yesterday? Can you remember everything or just some important things?

Activity

It's important to remember faces. Your brain is very good at it! Find pictures of ten faces. Show five of the faces quickly to a friend. Shuffle all ten faces together. Now spread them out. Can your friend remember which of the faces he or she has already seen?

89

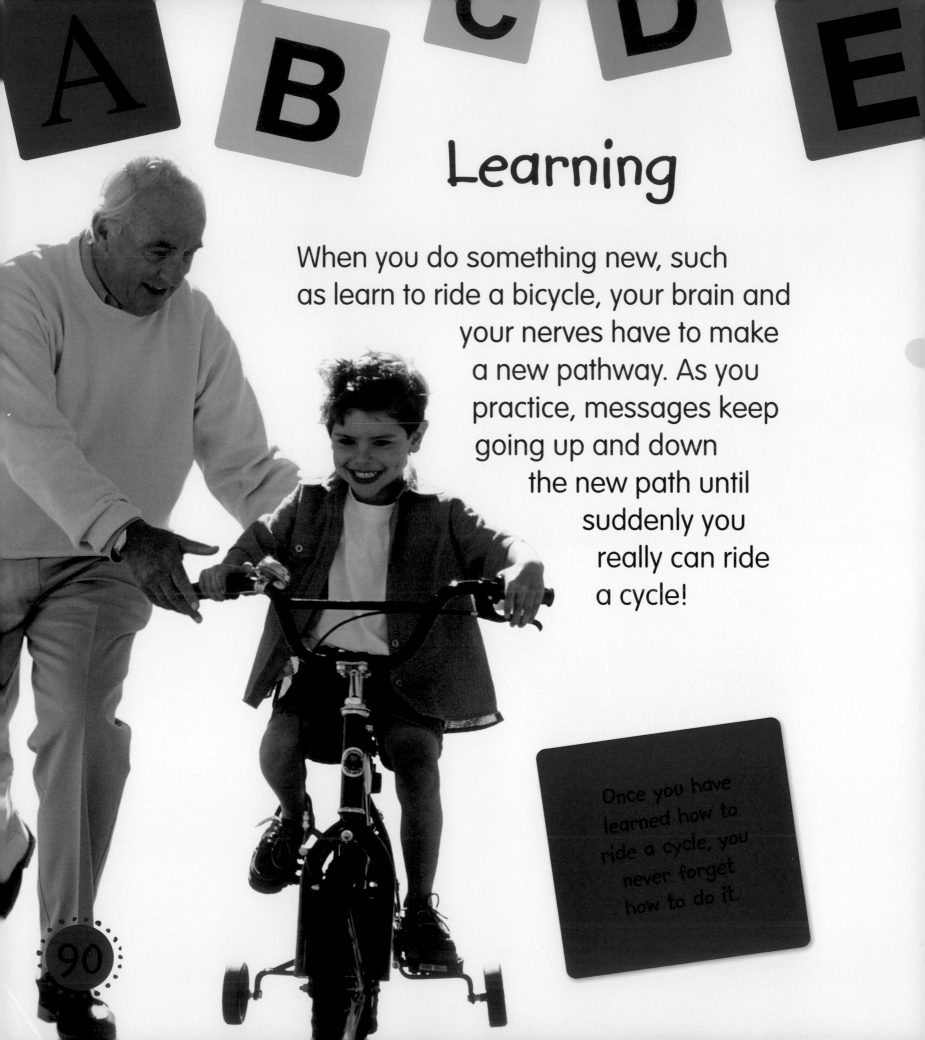

Learning

When you do something new, such as learn to ride a bicycle, your brain and your nerves have to make a new pathway. As you practice, messages keep going up and down the new path until suddenly you really can ride a cycle!

Once you have learned how to ride a cycle, you never forget how to do it.

90

Hard work and practice help you to learn new things, remember how to do them and get better at doing them.

Activity

Write your name with the hand you don't usually use. Practice over and over. Do you get better at writing with the "wrong" hand?

Kim

Kim

Kim

91

Feelings

How do you feel when you have been invited to a sleepover with your friends? How do you feel if someone borrows your favorite pen — then loses it? Do you feel excited, angry, sad, happy?

Your feelings come from your brain.

Activity

With your friend, think of a feeling, then pull a face and make your body show that feeling. Can your friend guess what the feeling is just by looking at you?

Feelings can help you to do the right thing at the right time.

If you feel afraid of a fierce animal, you keep away from it.

BEWARE OF THE DOG

If you feel happy to see your friend, you smile and your friend smiles back. You both feel happy and have a good time.

Healthy brain

Your brain is part of your body. There are lots of things you can do to keep it healthy.

Eat healthy food. Fruit, fish, vegetables and milk are all good for your brain, and for the rest of your body.

Keep your brain busy. Learn new things, play games and do puzzles.

Having fun and chatting with friends is good for your brain.

Sports and exercise are good for your whole body, including your brain.

Your brain does not need to work as hard when you are asleep, so get plenty of sleep and let it rest.

Why do you sleep?

You sleep because you get tired. Sleeping rests your body, especially your muscles.

When you are really tired, your eyes want to close.

If you sleep well, you wake up feeling refreshed and full of energy.

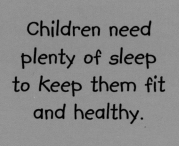

Children need plenty of sleep to keep them fit and healthy.

Sleeping rests your mind as well as your body. You are not aware of anything when you are deeply asleep because part of your brain is resting, too.

Monday 7:30 a.m.
Woke up by myself

Tuesday 7:40 a.m.
Woken up by Mom

Wednesday 7:30 a.m.
Woken up by Mom

Thursday 7:30 a.m.
Woke up by myself

Activity

If you sleep well, you should wake up easily in the morning. Keep a diary to show whether or not you woke up by yourself.

What happens when you sleep?

Some parts of your body never sleep. For example, your **heart** keeps beating, but more slowly. The parts of your brain that control your heart and breathing go on working, too.

Some parts of the body, such as the brain, work while you are awake and asleep.

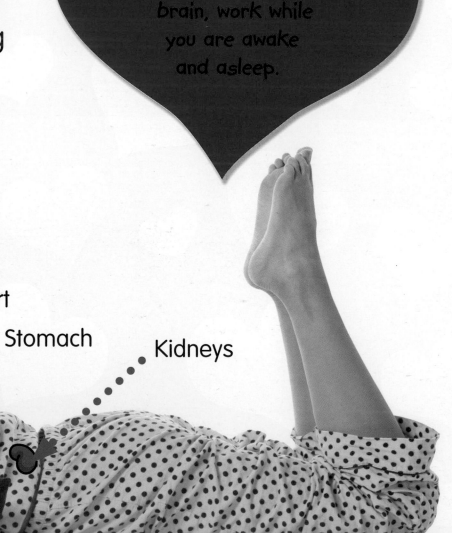

Brain

Lungs

Heart

Stomach

Kidneys

Your sleep changes during the night. At first, you sleep deeply. In the early morning, you sleep lightly and have **dreams**.

This graph shows how long you might spend in different kinds of sleep.

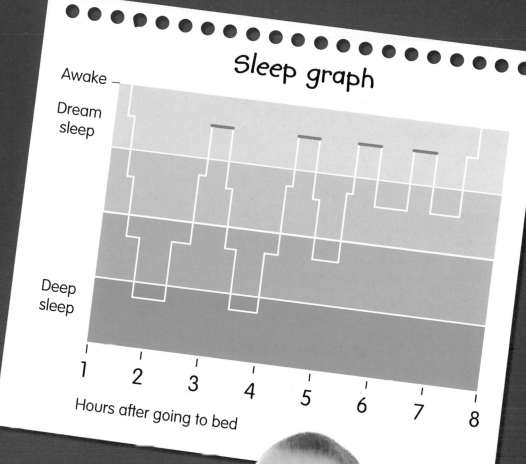

Sleep graph

Awake

Dream sleep

Deep sleep

1 2 3 4 5 6 7 8

Hours after going to bed

Activity

Sit cross-legged with your hands on your knees. Shut your eyes and breathe in and out slowly. Don't think of anything except your breathing. This will calm your mind and slow down your heartbeat.

Dreams

Dreams are like stories that come into your mind when you are asleep. You have about five dreams every night. You are most likely to remember a dream if you wake up in the middle of it.

Some dreams are about impossible things, such as flying.

100

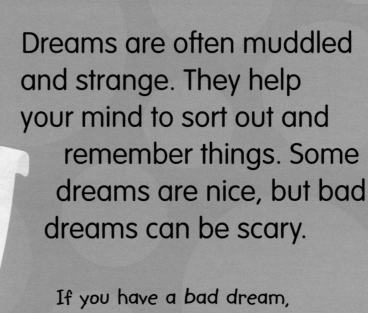

Dreams are often muddled and strange. They help your mind to sort out and remember things. Some dreams are nice, but bad dreams can be scary.

If you have a bad dream, remember that dreams are not real, and they stop once you have woken up.

Activity

Think of a dream that you remember. Tell your friends about it. Then listen to your friends' dreams.

A good night's sleep

Most children should sleep for about
10 or 11 hours every night. Children need
more sleep than adults because their
minds and bodies are still growing.

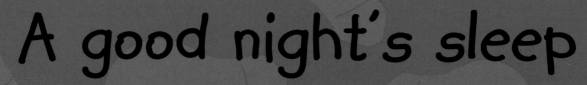

You are most likely to
sleep well if your
bedroom is
quiet and dark.

You should go to bed and get up at about the same time each day. Your brain then gets used to falling asleep at that time. Make sure your bed is comfortable and not full of toys.

Activity

Keep a diary for a week of the times you go to bed and get up. How long did you sleep each night?

Too little sleep

Sleep rests your mind. If you do not get enough sleep at night, you will feel tired during the day. You may be more grumpy, too.

When you are tired, you often yawn. This tells you that it's time to get some sleep.

It is harder for your brain to work well when you are tired. You may work more slowly or make lots of mistakes.

If you are tired at school, it will be more difficult to remember what you learn.

Activity

If you find it hard to go to sleep, try having a warm drink, such as hot chocolate or camomile tea. Do not drink too much though!

105

Notes for parents and teachers

1. Point out that people are animals called humans and that all animals have brains. Try to think of another animal that can talk. You could discuss the difference between a parrot talking and a human talking. Are there any other animals that can read and write?

2. Identify where your brain is. Talk about your skull, how it is hard and strong and the best shape to protect your brain. Look at a picture of the nervous system. Feel each other's spine and talk about how it is like a tube with the spinal cord running through the middle.

3. Talk about how the brain lets us sense the world around us. You can point to the parts of the body you use to see, hear, taste, smell and touch.

4. Play memory games together and exercise your brains. For example, say, "I went shopping and I bought some bread." The child repeats the item and adds a new one. "I went shopping and I bought some bread and some honey." Keep going and see how long your list can grow. The game stops when one of you forgets an item.

5. Learn something new together, maybe a poem or a new activity, such as juggling or a tune on the recorder. Talk about what you find hard and what you find easy when learning something new.

6. Talk to your child about how their body and mind needs to rest and recover at night. Sleeping helps them to be energetic and alert during the day. It also helps their bodies to fight off germs.

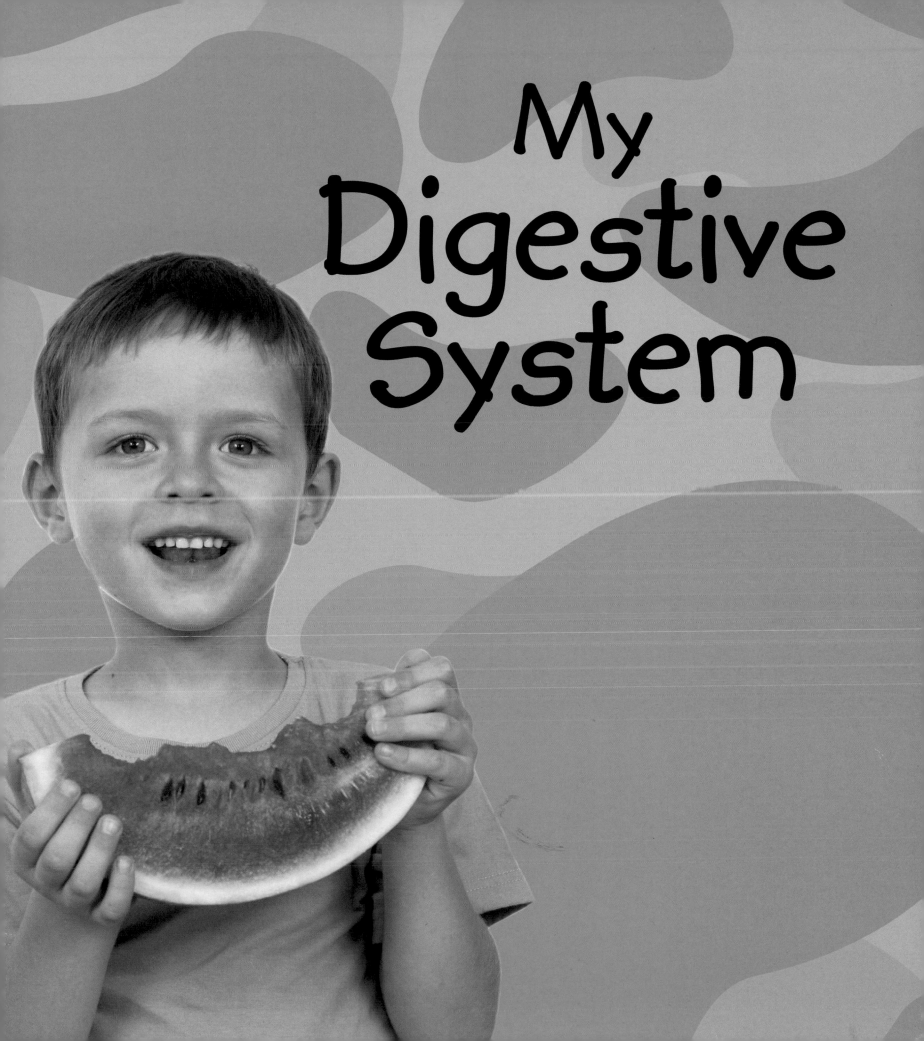

My
Digestive
System

What is your digestive system?

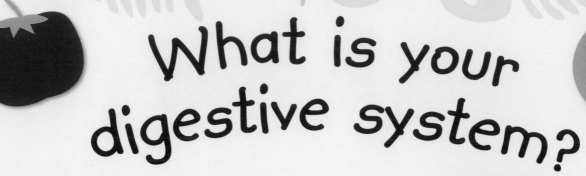

When you eat, your food goes on a journey through your **digestive system**.

On the way, your body takes nutrients (the bits that are good for you) from the food. Then, your body gets rid of the bits it can't use.

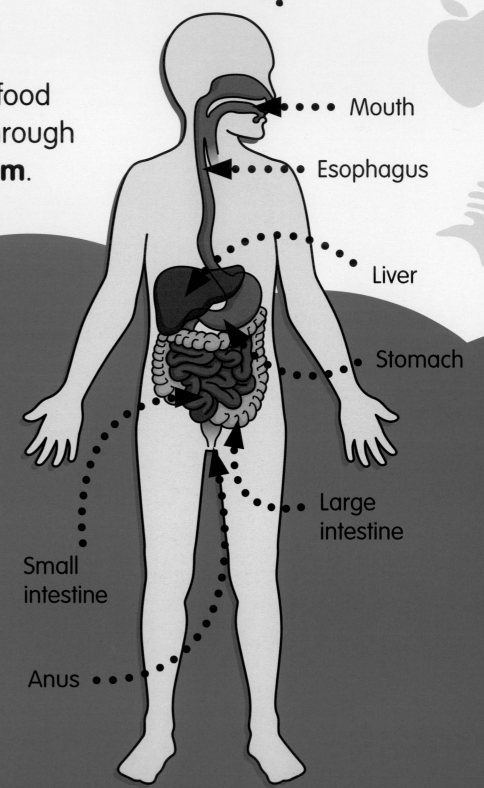

Mouth

Esophagus

Liver

Stomach

Large intestine

Small intestine

Anus

The journey is 21 feet long and takes about two days. The longest part of your digestive system is the small intestine. It is all curled up inside you.

Activity

You need a ball of string and some scissors. Use the string to measure 21 lengths of your adult shoe. Cut the string and stretch it out. This is about how far your food travels!

Food

Food gives you the **energy** you need to work and grow. It also helps you to keep warm and healthy. You need to eat something from each of these different food groups every day.

Fish, meat, eggs and nuts help your body to grow and **heal**.

Bread, cereal and pasta give you the energy you need to keep you going all day.

Milk, cheese, butter and cream help to build strong bones and give you energy.

Fruit and vegetables are full of **vitamins** and **minerals** that help to keep you healthy. They are full of fiber, the rough part of food that helps your body to get rid of waste.

You only need a little sugar and salt in your food, but it is important to drink plenty of water.

Mouth

Your food begins its journey in your mouth.

Seeing and smelling delicious food makes you want to eat. When you put food in your mouth, you taste its flavor with the tiny taste buds on your tongue.

Activity

Smell your favorite dinner cooking. Feel your mouth water. It is filling with saliva ready for eating!

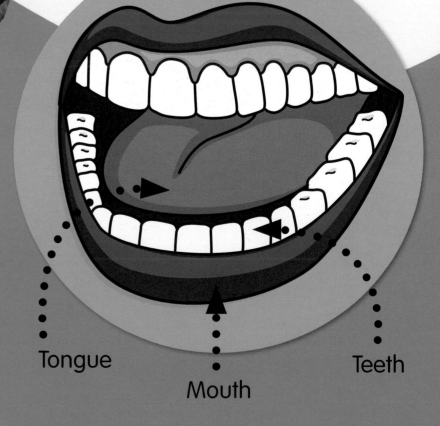

Tongue

Mouth

Teeth

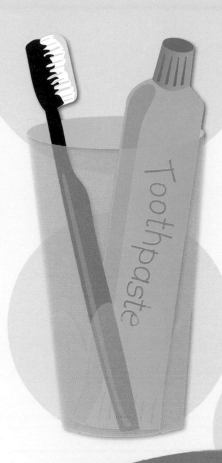

You chew your food into small pieces with your teeth. Your front teeth are for biting. Your back teeth are for chewing.

Look after your teeth. You need them for eating!

Saliva helps to make your food slippery so you can swallow it easily. Your tongue helps you to swallow your food.

Esophagus

When you swallow a mouthful of chewed-up food,
it goes down a tube called the esophagus
(say *ee-sof-agus*). Your esophagus is next to your
windpipe, which carries air to your lungs.

A little flap over your windpipe stops
food going down it.

If you eat too fast
and you cough, we say your
food has "gone down the
wrong way." That means,
it has gone down your
windpipe by mistake! Try
to eat slowly to
avoid choking!

Your food doesn't slither straight down into your stomach. Muscles in your esophagus squeeze it down slowly.

When giraffes bend down to drink, muscles in their esophagus push the water upwards!

If you eat bad food, your body gets rid of it. Muscles squeeze the food back up again and you are sick.

Being sick or vomiting feels horrible, but it helps you to get better quickly.

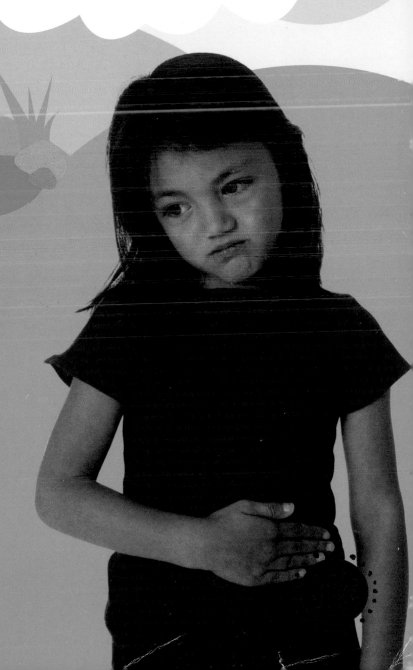

Stomach

Your esophagus pushes food into your stomach. Your stomach is a muscle. It is like a stretchy bag. It stretches when it is full of food.

Food stays in your stomach for about three hours while it is digested. "Digested" means that it is mixed and mashed up.

When your food has turned soft and runny like soup, it leaves your stomach. You start to feel **hungry** again when your stomach is empty.

Activity

Make a timetable of your meals. Notice the time when you feel hungry. Is it about three hours after your last meal? A healthy snack can stop you feeling hungry between meals.

Breakfast	8 o'clock
Lunch	12 o'clock
Supper	6 o'clock

Small intestine

Your food takes about four hours to ooze along your small intestine where it becomes even more runny and watery. Bubbles of gas in your intestines make a rumbling sound while your food is being digested.

Activity

Listen to tummy rumbles. When a friend's or one of your family's tummy rumbles loudly, ask if you can put your ear on their stomach and listen to their food being digested!

Food is full of "nutrients" or goodness that your body needs to grow, to keep healthy and to provide you with energy. While your food is in your small intestine, nutrients from your food go into your blood.

It's important to eat food full of the nutrients your body needs.

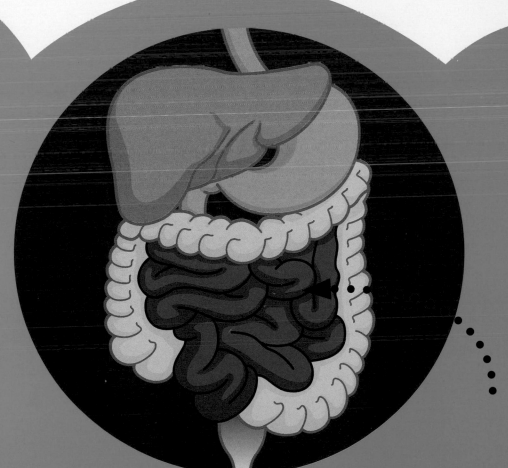

Your small intestine is longer than your large intestine. It is called small because it is narrow.

Small intestine

Liver and blood

Blood full of nutrients from your food goes to your liver. Your liver is the biggest organ in your body.

Your liver makes a special juice called bile, which breaks down food into things the body can use. It stores the nutrients and gets rid of the parts of food that are bad for you.

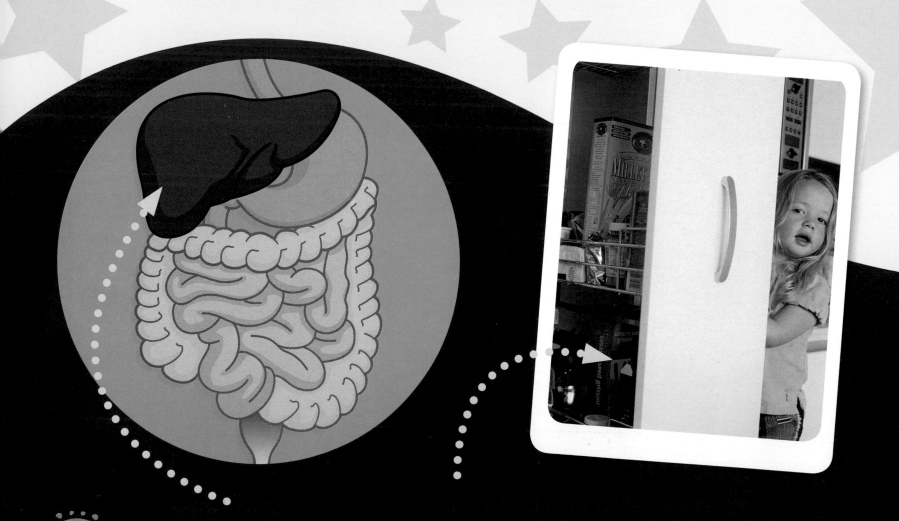

When your liver has done its job, it sends nutrients into your blood through your blood vessels.

Your blood delivers goodness from your food to every bit of your body.

121

Large intestine

When your food reaches the large intestine, it is mostly waste. Waste is the part of your food that your body doesn't need. It goes into the large intestine and stays there for about two days.

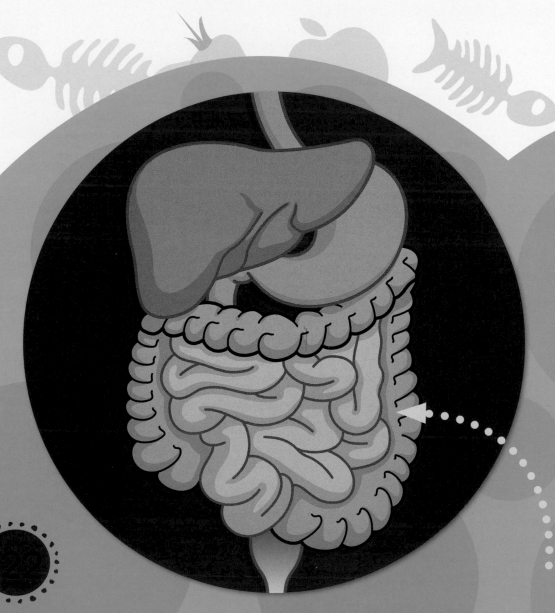

While your food is in your large intestine, the last little bit of nutrients and most of the water goes into your body. Your food is nearly at the end of its journey.

Large intestine

By the time the remains of your food reach the end of your large intestine, it has become "feces." Your body gets rid of feces through an opening called the anus.

Poo is what is left of your food after the goodness has been taken from it.

Healthy digestive system

There are lots of ways you can keep your digestive system healthy.

- Eat healthy food full of the nutrients your body needs.

- Drink plenty of water. Water helps food go through your digestive system.

Try to eat lots of fruit and vegetables. They are delicious and help to make you strong and healthy.

Fruit and vegetables are full of fiber.

Activity

Start the day with a breakfast that is good for your digestive system. Wash and grate an apple including the peel. Slice a banana. Add milk, a little lemon juice, honey and a sprinkle of oats. Mix it all together and eat up!

Notes for parents and teachers

1. Explain that we are a kind of animal called a human and that all animals need food and drink to stay alive. Find pictures of different animals and look at the food they eat.

2. Talk about how we all need energy to give us the power to work and play, and that food gives us energy. Discuss other kinds of energy, such as gasoline for cars, and electricity for light. What happens to us without food, to a car without gasoline and to a light without electricity?

3. Put out a variety of food and sort it into the main food groups. Discuss what is the same about the food in each group and talk about why your body needs each different kind of food.

4. Explain why it is so important to keep our teeth healthy. Eat a piece of crusty bread together. Point out how your front teeth bite, the pointed teeth tear and the back teeth chew. Notice how they are the right shape for the job they do. Talk about the kind of food we would have to eat if we didn't have teeth!

5. Draw a simple picture of the digestive system together. Trace the route your food takes. Name each part the food is going through and describe what is happening to the food. Use words such as chew, swallow, mix and mash.

My Skin

Keeping clean

Your hands and skin get dirty from all the things you touch during the day. Your fingers may get sticky with food, and your hands may get grubby from playing indoors or outside.

Your skin makes **sweat** to keep you cool. Sweat contains salt and other substances, which are left on your skin after the sweat has dried.

You need to wash your skin to wash away dirt, sweat and germs.

Some dirt contains **germs**. These are tiny living things that are too small to see. If they get inside your body, they can make you ill.

This child is muddy and sweaty from playing soccer.

129

Amazing skin

Pore

Sweat

Hair

Skin protects your body and keeps out dirt and germs. Skin is **waterproof** and stretchy. Most of your skin is covered with fine hairs.

The hairs on your skin help to keep you warm.

Our skin is waterproof, and so keeps water out of our bodies when we swim or bathe.

130

Old skin flakes off and is replaced by new skin. If your skin is cut or scraped, your body repairs the damage and new skin grows over the **wound**.

As a scrape heals, new skin grows under the scab.

Activity

Test a piece of cling wrap, a tissue and a bandage to see which is most like skin. Which one lets you bend your finger most easily? Which ones are waterproof?

Washing and drying

The best way to clean your hands is to wet them and rub soap all over them. Then rinse your hands in clean water and dry them carefully on a clean towel.

Towels

Nail brush

Bubble bath

Soap, bubble bath, a nail brush and towels can all be used to keep clean.

Hand soap

Activity

Mix some flour and water together with your hands to make a sticky dough. Rinse your hands in cold water. Now clean them using warm water, soap and a nailbrush. Which way works best?

If dirt gets stuck under your nails, clean them with a nailbrush. Have your nails cut from time to time. Short nails are less likely to get dirty.

Scrubbing your nails with a nailbrush is the best way to clean them.

Clean all over

You should bath or shower regularly so that your skin is clean all over. Otherwise, your skin could become itchy, and your feet might start to smell. Washing gets rid of dirt, sweat and old skin.

After bathing or showering, dry yourself carefully, especially between your toes.

Activity

Wash and rinse your hair, then run your fingers down a strand of hair. If it squeaks, it is clean. Clean hair is easy to brush.

Wash your hair with shampoo at least once a week. If you don't, your head could become itchy. Conditioner helps to make your hair shiny and easy to comb.

Shampoo cleans your hair and the skin on your head.

Bacteria and viruses

Bacteria and **viruses** are different kinds of germs. If they get inside your body, some of them can make you ill.

Usually bacteria are too small to see. This photo shows what bacteria look like.

Activity

Use a hand mirror to look inside your mouth. Can you see any germs? They are there even though you cannot see them. Your saliva will kill most of them.

136

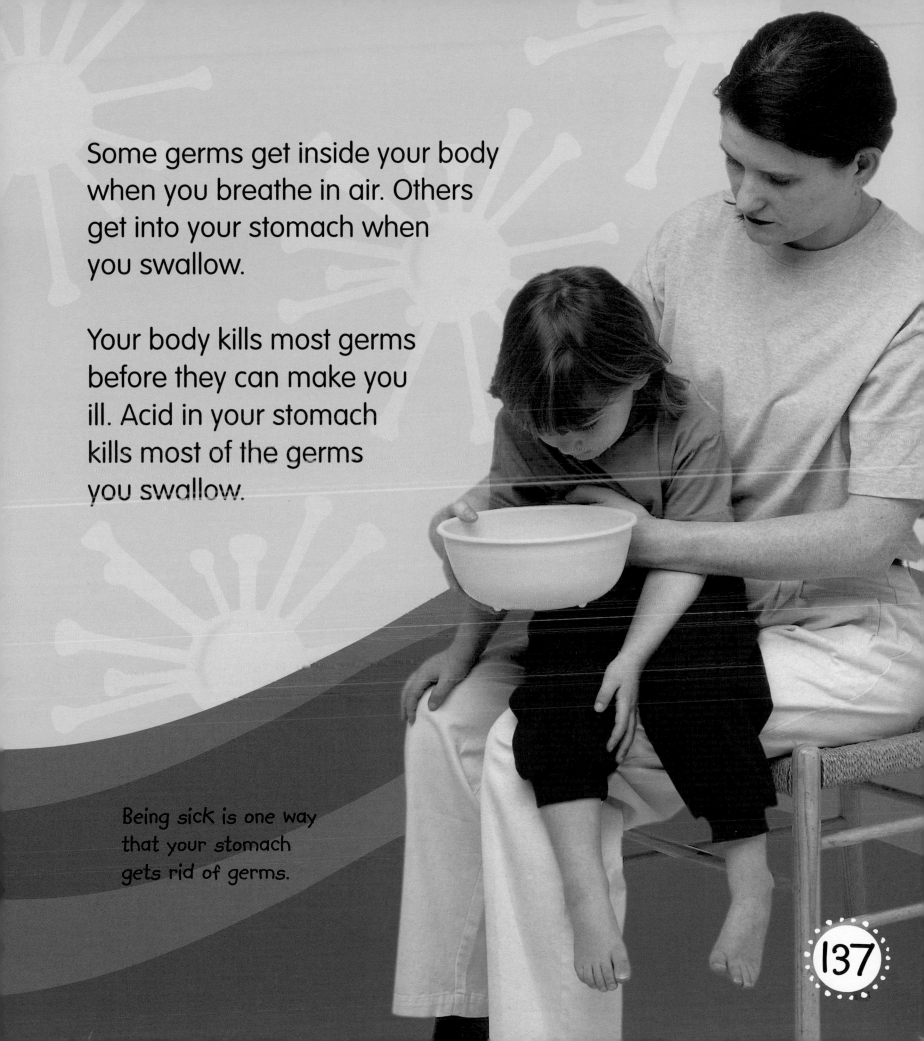

Some germs get inside your body when you breathe in air. Others get into your stomach when you swallow.

Your body kills most germs before they can make you ill. Acid in your stomach kills most of the germs you swallow.

Being sick is one way that your stomach gets rid of germs.

137

Don't swallow germs

If you touch something with germs on it, some of the germs will stick to your fingers. When you use your fingers to eat something, some of the germs could go into your mouth, and then into your stomach.

Germs on your hands can rub off onto your food.

Activity

Suck a lollipop until it is sticky. Take it out of your mouth and sprinkle it with some flour. Does it stick to the lollipop? This shows how easily germs stick to things.

138

Keep germs out of your mouth by always washing your hands before you eat. Wash unpeeled fruit before you eat it, too.

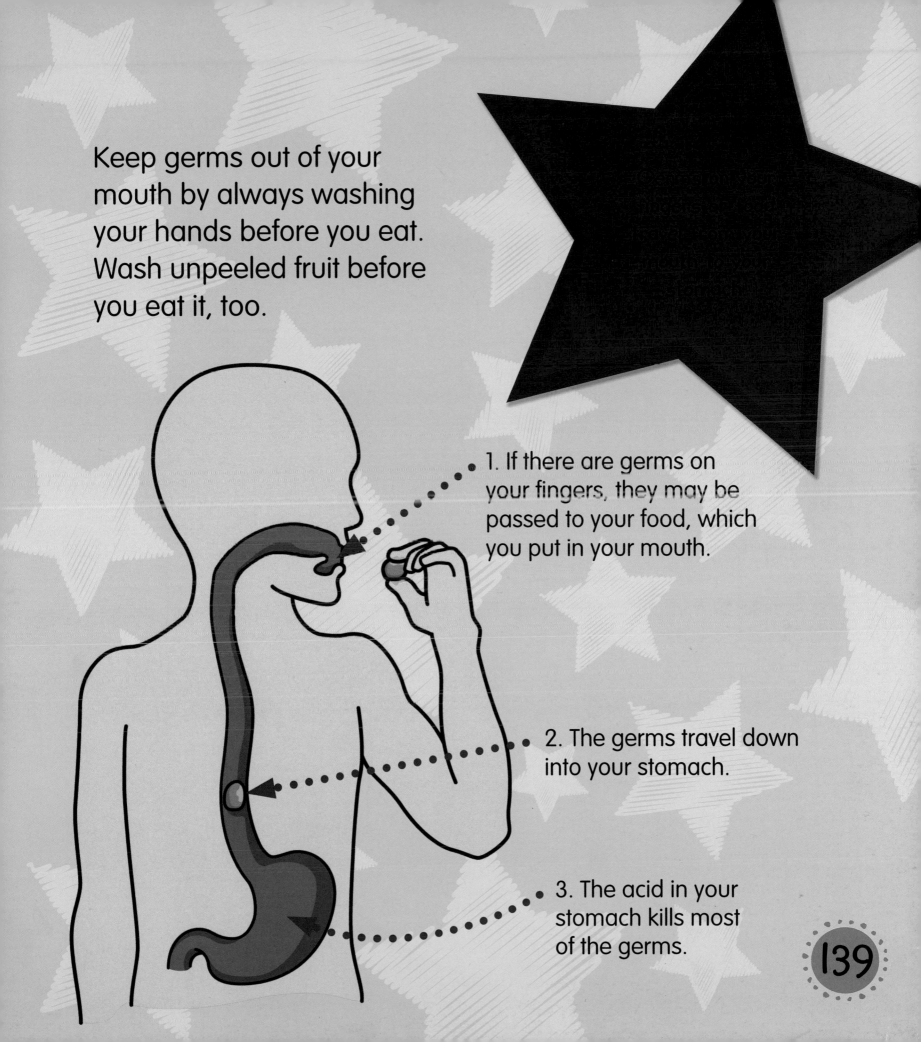

1. If there are germs on your fingers, they may be passed to your food, which you put in your mouth.

2. The germs travel down into your stomach.

3. The acid in your stomach kills most of the germs.

Flush and wash!

Poo contains millions of germs. These germs stick to surfaces around the toilet. Some of them can get on your hands.

You should always wash your hands after you have used the toilet. If you don't, the germs can move from your hands into your mouth when you eat. These germs can make you sick or give you bad tummy ache.

Use soap and water to wash your hands well after using the toilet.

Activity

Mix up some powder paint and water. Cover your hands with paint and then press them onto a big sheet of paper. How many handprints can you make? This shows how paint (and germs) cling to your skin.

Don't pass on germs

Coughs and colds pass easily from one person to another. When you cough or sneeze, millions of germs shoot into the air. Other people could then breathe in some of your germs.

Sneezing can spread germs in the air.

When you blow your nose or sneeze, lots of germs get onto your fingers. You could leave germs on everything you touch. Stop this from happening by using a tissue when you sneeze.

Used tissues should always be thrown away into a covered trash can.

Activity

If you sneeze, cover your nose. If you cough, cover your mouth. Wash your hands, too, so that you do not pass on your germs.

Cuts and scrapes

Germs can also get inside your body if your skin is scratched or broken. If a wound bleeds, the blood helps to wash away germs and dirt. However, you still need to wash the wound carefully.

When the wound is clean, dry it carefully. Cover it with a bandage to stop germs getting in. Then the wound will begin to heal itself.

A bandage keeps a cut clean until it begins to heal.

Activity

If you scratch or graze your skin, keep a diary of what happens to it as it heals. How long does it take for the scab to fall off?

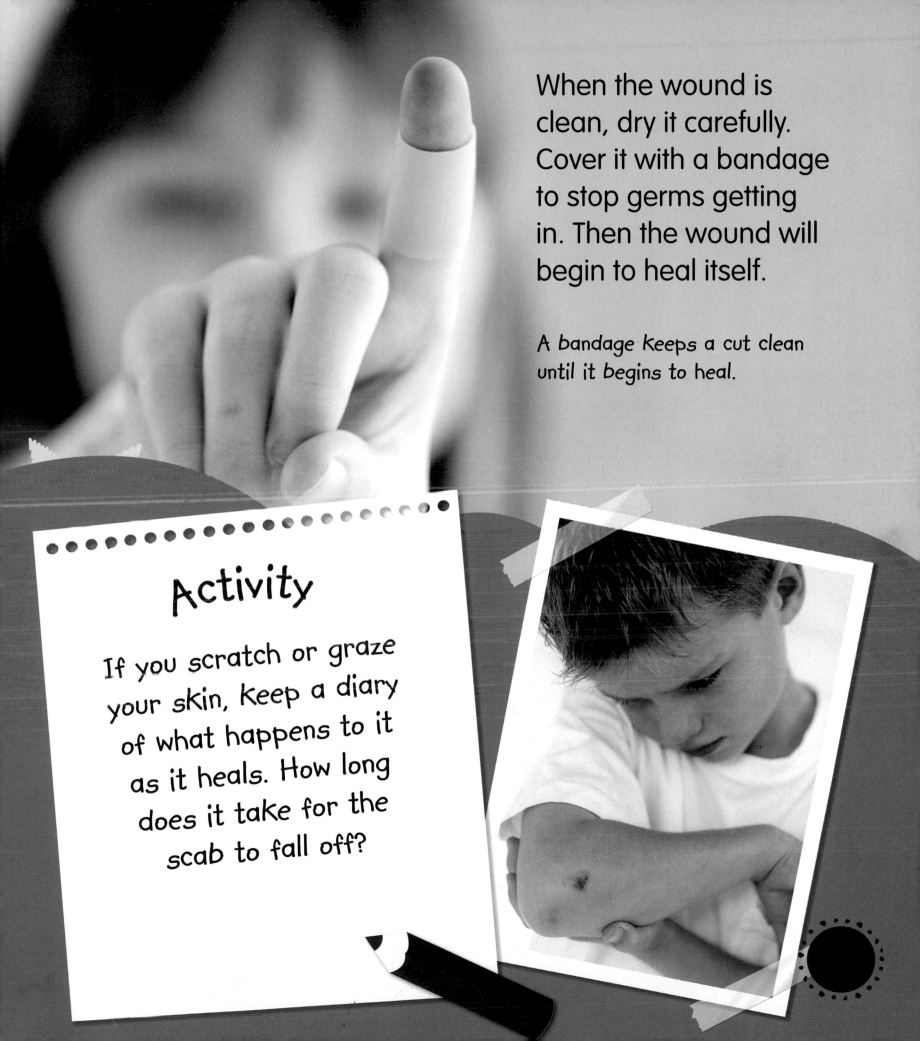

Notes for parents and teachers

1. Encourage the children to take an interest in their own health. Talk to them about the importance of washing their hands, particularly before eating and after using the toilet.

2. Make washing more interesting by collecting a selection of fun soaps in different colors, shapes and smells. Bubble bath makes bathing more fun, too.

3. Experiment with soap bubbles. Run a bowl of warm water and add dishwashing liquid. Agitate the water to make it foamy. Show the children how to make a bubble by rubbing your thumb against your forefinger and then touching the tip of your thumb to the tip of your finger to make a circle of soapy water. Blow the water to form the bubble. Who can make the biggest bubble?

4. Encourage the children to be aware of food hygiene. Show them how to separate uncooked meat, for example, from other food in the refrigerator. Encourage them to check the "use by" dates on food, such as fruit yogurts and smoothies, before eating them.

5. Wash or peel fruit and vegetables, such as apples and carrots, before children eat them. Ask the children to help you to wash grapes, cherries, strawberries and other fruits.

6. Talk about germs and how small they are. If you are going on a picnic or somewhere where you cannot wash your hands before eating, use antibacterial gel instead.

Glossary

Alive You are alive, and so are plants and animals. Things that are alive grow, move, eat and can sense what is going on around them.

Bacteria Germs are made of tiny bacteria. Bacteria cause illnesses such as ear infections and stomach aches. Medicines called antibiotics are used to kill bacteria.

Blood The red liquid that runs through your blood vessels to every part of your body is called blood. It carries goodness from your food and oxygen from your lungs.

Blood vessels Tubes that carry your blood are called blood vessels. Arteries carry blood away from your heart. Veins carry blood back to your heart.

Bone There are 206 bones in your body. They are joined together to make up your skeleton.

Brain Your brain is inside your head and controls every part of your body. Most of the brain goes on working when you are asleep, but the part that makes you aware of what is happening around you "switches off."

Breathe You breathe air in and out of your lungs. You breathe through your nose and mouth.

Calcium The substance that makes your teeth and bones hard and strong. Some foods also contain calcium, such as cheese and milk.

Coordination The ability to make your muscles and senses work together at the right time. When you catch a ball, your eyes track the path of the ball. Your muscles then move your hands to catch it.

Dentine The main part of a tooth is made of dentine. It is similar to bone and is covered with a layer of very hard enamel.

Digestive system Your digestive system is all the parts of your body that work together to digest your food.

Dreams You have dreams as you sleep. You see, feel and hear things that seem to be real, but are not actually happening. When you dream, your eyes flicker, even though your eyelids are shut.

Enamel The hard, glossy outer layer of a tooth. Enamel contains calcium and fluoride. It is the strongest substance in the body.

Energy You need energy to give you the power to work. Food gives you energy.

Exercise Moving about, for example running, swimming, jumping, stretching and skipping, is exercise. It helps to keep your body strong and healthy.

Germs All germs are tiny living things. They are so small that you need a microscope to see them. Germs include bacteria and viruses. They can make you ill if they get inside your body. Germs can pass from one person to another.

Heal Your body heals or gets better when you cut yourself or when you are ill.

Heart The part of your body that pumps blood to your lungs and around your body. Your heart is in your chest. Your heart beats more slowly when you are asleep. It beats fastest when you are most active.

Hungry You feel hungry when your stomach is empty. Feeling hungry makes you want to eat.

Joint Where two bones meet. Most of your joints can move. Your elbows and knees are joints.

Messages Facts and information sent from one place to another. Messages are sent along your nerves to your brain. If you see a bird, a message goes from your eyes to your brain. Your brain tells you "bird."

Minerals Minerals are tiny parts of goodness in food. Minerals in milk help you build strong teeth and bones.

Muscles Your muscles pull your bones so you can move. Muscles keep your heart beating and your lungs breathing.

Nerves Your nerves are like paths running from your brain to every part of your body. Messages are sent back and forth along your nerves.

Oxygen One of the gases in the air. Blood picks up oxygen from the air you breathe into your lungs. Your heart then pumps the blood to every part of your body.

Plaque A sticky substance that is made by bacteria in your mouth. Plaque contains acid that can cause tooth decay. Cleaning your teeth helps to remove plaque and stop it forming.

Protect This means to keep something safe from being hurt. Your skull protects your brain.

Pulp This is the soft material in the center of a tooth. It includes blood vessels and nerves.

Pump A pump pushes liquid along. Your heart is a pump that pushes blood through your blood vessels.

Relax When you relax, you rest and become calmer. You relax your body when you rest your muscles. You relax your mind when you do something quiet and soothing.

Remember When you learn a new skill, you remember it. You don't forget it and you don't have to learn it again.

Routine A routine is a regular way of doing the same things every day at the same time.

Saliva A liquid like water in your mouth is called saliva. It helps you to taste and swallow your food.

Senses You have five senses — sight, touch, taste, smell and hearing. They give you information about what is going on around you.

Shape Everything has a shape. For example, a ball is a round shape. Your skeleton gives your body its shape.

Skull Your skull is the framework of bones in your head that protects your brain. It is sometimes called your brain box.

Stamina The ability to keep going without running out of breath when you are exercising. If you have plenty of stamina, your lungs can take in a lot of air without you having to breathe very fast, and your heart can pump a lot of blood around your body without having to beat very fast.

Support When you hold something upright or stop it from falling, you are giving support.

Sweat The salty water that oozes out through tiny holes in your skin when you are hot is called sweat.

Tooth decay A tooth decays when part of it rots. Tooth decay begins when acid in the mouth eats a hole in the enamel of a tooth. If it spreads to the soft pulp in the center of the tooth, it can be very painful.

Virus A virus is a kind of germ. Viruses cause illnesses such as colds and flu. Antibiotic medicines do not kill viruses.

Vitamins Tiny parts of goodness in food are called vitamins. Vitamins in fruit help to keep your skin healthy.

Waterproof Something is waterproof when it does not let any water through it

Windpipe Your windpipe is the tube that carries air into your lungs when you breathe in, and carries it out again when you breathe out.

Wound Your body is wounded when your skin is damaged or cut.

Index